BEST EDITORIAL CARTOONS OF THE YEAR

1987 EDITION

Edited by
CHARLES BROOKS

Foreword by CHARLES ROBB

PELICAN PUBLISHING COMPANY

GRETNA 1987

Library of Congress Serial Catalog Data

Best editorial cartoons. 1972-
Gretna [La.] Pelican Pub. Co.
v. 29 cm. annual-
"A pictorial history of the year."

1. United States- Politics and government—
1969—Caricatures and Cartoons—Periodicals.
E839.5.B45   320.9'7309240207   73-643645
ISSN 0091-2220   MARC-S

Manufactured in the United States of America
Published by Pelican Publishing Company, Inc.
1101 Monroe Street, Gretna, Louisiana 70053

Contents

DICK GIBSON
Courtesy Toronto Sun

Foreword

If the job of editorial writers is to shoot the wounded, then editorial cartoonists must have been created to cremate the remains. Like most others who have held public office, I can speak from intensely personal experience. In fact, I'd be willing to bet that even my childhood dentist could learn new things about torture from political cartoonists.

Inevitably, "Death by Cartoon" occurs just as some embarrassing crisis reaches its darkest hour. The method of execution is always the same: lethal injections of printer's ink from a cartoonist's sharpest pen. And for those whose ox happens to have been gored in

DEATH BY CARTOON

7

FOREWORD

the process, the memory of these public embalmings lingers long after the crisis is otherwise forgotten. In fact, it may be that the only thing all politicians can agree upon—regardless of party or philosophy—is the collective empathy we feel for others who have borne the brunt of your exquisite torture.

I've even heard of a politician who yearned to effect a hostile take-over of a particular newspaper so that he could personally fire the cartoonist and his editor on their birthdays. And in our heart of hearts, all of us would secretly like revenge for the cruel and unusual ways you thin our hairlines, fatten our waistlines and double our chins! (And, of course, we want you to continue to let us have your original artwork when you flatter us!)

In our sober and reflective moments, however, those of us in public life realize the importance of your work, and—in theory at least—we are grateful for your skills in puncturing the pompous and humbling the mighty. Every public official needs the healthy fear that comes from knowing that his or her every action is subject to a visual ridicule that the man in the street can understand. We recognize that your work can accentuate the positive as well as display the negative, and we are ever mindful of the inspiration that David Low's cartoons gave Britain as she faced Hitler alone or the comforting realism that Bill Mauldin's Joe and Willie provided to the average GI in World War II.

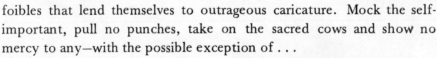

So keep your wits and pens sharp and continue to cast your keen eyes on the personal foibles that lend themselves to outrageous caricature. Mock the self-important, pull no punches, take on the sacred cows and show no mercy to any—with the possible exception of . . .

Your humble servant,

Charles S. Robb
Governor of Virginia (1982-86)

Award-Winning Cartoons

1986 PULITZER PRIZE

FEIFFER®

JULES FEIFFER
Cartoonist
Universal Press Syndicate

Born in the Bronx, New York, 1929; attended Pratt Institute; author of ten volumes of collected cartoons, including *Feiffer on Nixon;* author of four plays, two screenplays, and two novels; the only cartoonist to have a comic strip published by the *New York Times;* cartoonist for *The Village Voice;* syndicated by Universal Press Syndicate.

1985 SIGMA DELTA CHI AWARD
(Selected in 1986)

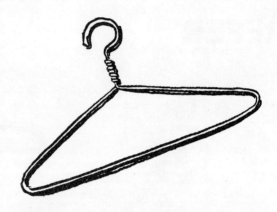

DOUG MARLETTE
Editorial Cartoonist
Charlotte Observer

Born in Greensboro, North Carolina; began newspaper cartoon career at age 16; attended Florida State University, majoring in philosophy and minoring in art; editorial cartoonist for the Charlotte *Observer,* 1972 to present; syndicated to more than 100 newspapers through the Tribune Media Services; the only cartoonist to be awarded a Nieman Fellowship at Harvard; creator of the syndicated comic strip "Kudzu."

1986 NATIONAL HEADLINERS CLUB AWARD

MIKE KEEFE
Editorial Cartoonist
Denver Post

Born November 6, 1946 in Santa Rosa, California; earned two degrees in mathematics from the University of Missouri at Kansas City, where he also completed the coursework for a doctorate; editorial cartoonist for the Denver *Post*, 1975 to present; syndicated nationally by News America Syndicate; co-creator, with Tim Menees, of the comic strip "Cooper," which is distributed by Universal Press Syndicate.

1986 FISCHETTI AWARD

DOUG MARLETTE
Editorial Cartoonist
Charlotte Observer

1985 NATIONAL NEWSPAPER AWARD/CANADA
(Selected in 1986)

ED FRANKLIN
Editorial Cartoonist
Toronto Globe and Mail

Illustrator and cartoonist for the *Globe* and *Mail* since 1968; studied art at the Pratt Institute in New York, where he later worked as an illustrator; also served as cartoonist for the Houston *Press* and the Houston *Post*.

Best Editorial Cartoons of the Year

BILL GARNER
Courtesy Washington Times

The Reagan Administration

The business dealings of Michael Deaver, deputy chief of staff during President Reagan's first term, caused the White House political problems and raised serious conflict of interest questions. There were numerous allegations that Deaver, who left the White House in 1985 to start his own public relations firm, had used his closeness to Reagan to profit handsomely. A three-judge panel was named to supervise an investigation into Deaver's lobbying activities, and a federal grand jury was convened to look into perjury allegations against Deaver.

The media reacted angrily to reports that the Reagan Administration had given the press false information concerning Libya and its leader, Moammar Qaddafi. According to the reports, the White House "disinformation" program was intended to persuade Qaddafi that the U.S. was preparing to invade Libya. Bernard Kalb, assistant secretary of state for public affairs, resigned in protest of the alleged campaign.

Vice President George Bush set off a controversy on a visit to Saudi Arabia in the spring when he was quoted as saying that oil prices were dropping too fast and that the oil markets needed stability. The Saudis and Bush's home state of Texas, a major oil producer, may have been pleased by his remarks, but they incensed many Americans who still had memories of the escalating oil prices of a few years ago.

ED STEIN
Courtesy Rocky Mountain News

DRAPER HILL
Courtesy Detroit News

WALT HANDELSMAN
Courtesy Scranton Times

PAUL SZEP
Courtesy Boston Globe

DAVID HORSEY
Courtesy Seattle Post–Intelligencer

The Reagan Safety Net

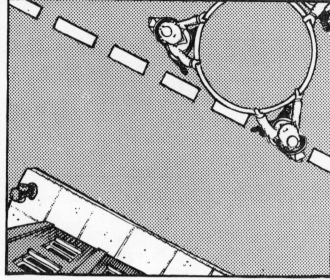

H. CLAY BENNETT
Courtesy St. Petersburg Times

MILT PRIGGEE
Courtesy Dayton Journal–Herald

DESIGNING AMERICAN FOREIGN POLICY

PAUL FELL
Courtesy Lincoln (Neb.) Journal

ASK THE JUDGE IF DISINFORMATION COUNTS.

JACK LANIGAN
Courtesy New Bedford
Standard Times

BRUCE BEATTIE
Courtesy Daytona Beach
News–Journal

©86 Daytona Beach News-Journal
Copley News Service

"Look! Another disinformation campaign!"

V. CULLUM ROGERS
Courtesy Durham Morning Herald

MIKE GRASTON
Courtesy Windsor Star (Ont.)

Berry's World

"Actually, I peddle access to MIKE DEAVER."

JIM BERRY
© NEA

King of the lobbyists and coin of the realm

MICHAEL K. DEAVER

BILL MITCHELL
Courtesy Potomac News

MICHAEL K. DEAVER & ASSOCIATES

GARNER © .86
THE WASHINGTON TIMES

BILL GARNER
Courtesy Washington Times

Iranian Arms Deal

The year's top news story broke in November when it was revealed that the U.S. had sent military equipment to Iran, a long-time bitter enemy. President Reagan admitted the sale, contending it was an effort to foster better relations with Iran because of its strategic location. He vigorously denied that the weapons had been sent as ransom for American hostages being held by pro-Iranian groups in Lebanon. Critics in the U.S. and around the world expressed disbelief, however, when shortly afterward captive David Jacobsen was released. The Reagan Administration had insisted it would never link hostage safety to political concessions, and it appeared to most Americans as a major change in policy.

On November 25 the White House announced that some $30 million in profits from the Iranian arms sale had been channeled by the National Security Council to the Contras fighting to overthrow the Sandinista government in Nicaragua. Congress had cut back sharply on aid to the Contras, and a howl of protest went up from both Republicans and Democrats over the disclosure.

As more allegations came to light, Reagan dismissed Lt. Col. Oliver North, who was alleged to have engineered the transfer of funds through the National Security Council. Even while firing North, Reagan characterized him as an American hero. North's boss, White House National Security Adviser John Poindexter, submitted his resignation and investigations of the affair sprang up all over Washington.

MIKE KEEFE
Courtesy Denver Post

BOB TAYLOR
Courtesy Dallas Times–Herald

DICK LOCHER
Courtesy Chicago Tribune

JERRY BYRD
Courtesy Beaumont Enterprise

ROY PETERSON
Courtesy Vancouver Sun

CHUCK AYERS
Courtesy Akron Beacon–Journal

25

"....REPEAT, EVERYTHING IS UNDER CONTROL!......(NOW, WHERE'S THE REVERSE ON THIS THING?!)....."

"IT'S OUR POLICY TO NEVER NEGOTIATE WITH TERRORISTS!.....HE, ON THE OTHER HAND, WAS ONLY A MIDDLEMAN."

LAMBERT DER
Courtesy Greenville News-Piedmont

DICK WALLMEYER
Courtesy Independent Press–Telegram
(Calif.)

DAVID WILEY MILLER
Courtesy San Francisco Examiner

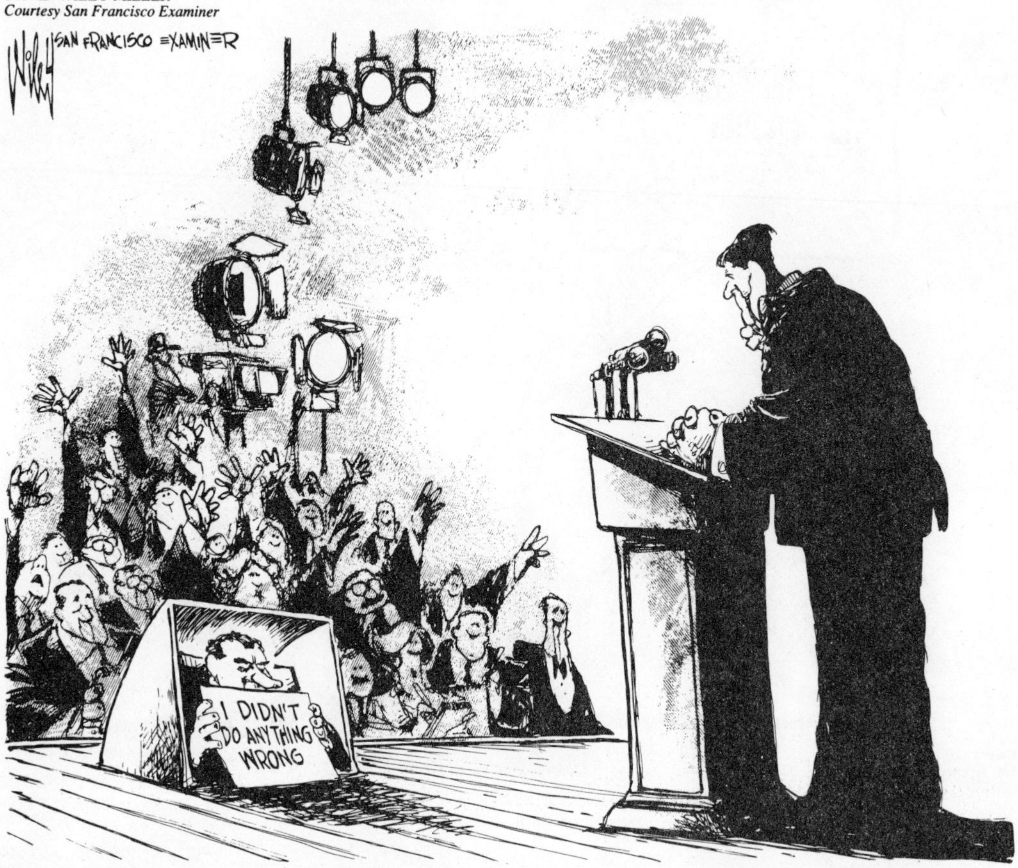
WILEY SAN FRANCISCO EXAMINER
I DIDN'T DO ANYTHING WRONG

JACK HIGGINS
Courtesy Chicago Sun–Times

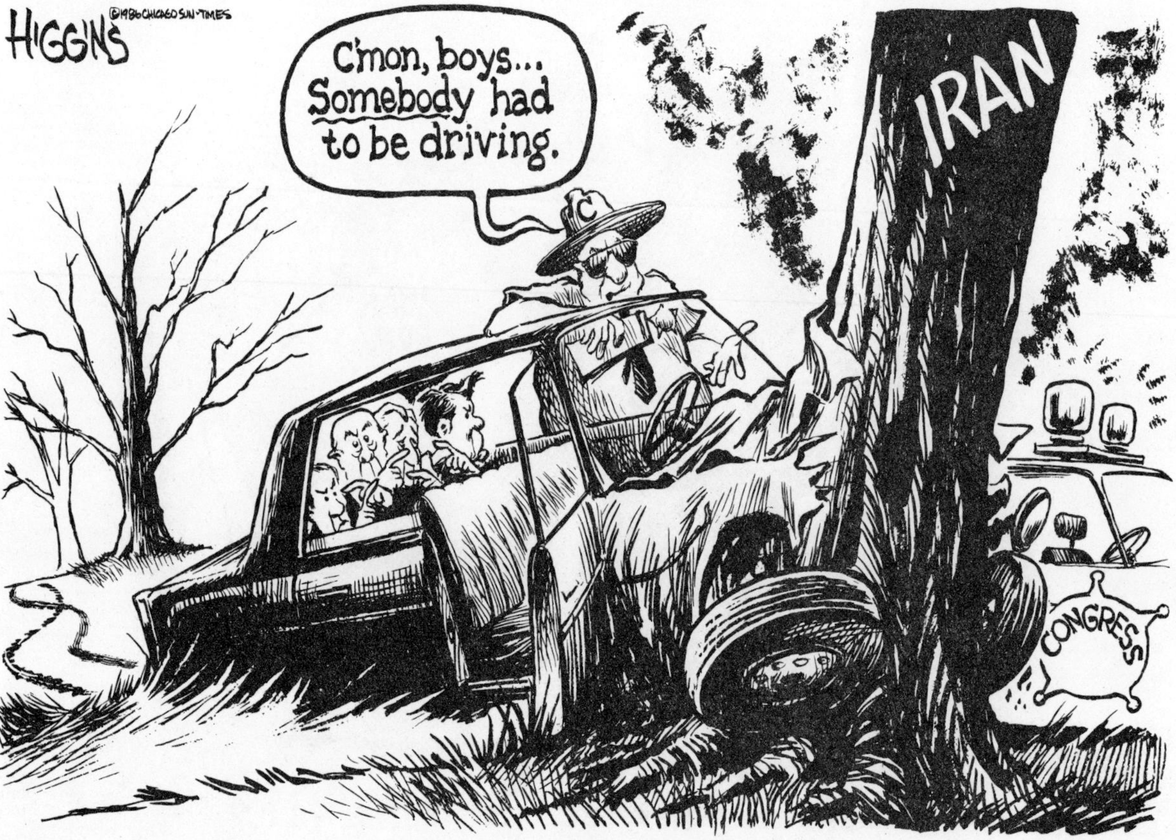
HIGGINS ©1986 CHICAGO SUN-TIMES
C'mon, boys... Somebody had to be driving.
IRAN
C
CONGRESS

DAVID WILEY MILLER
Courtesy San Francisco Examiner

JERRY FEARING
*Courtesy St. Paul Dispatch–
Pioneer Press*

LAZARO FRESQUET
Courtesy El Miami Herald

SAM RAWLS
Courtesy Atlanta Constitution

JACK MCLEOD
© Army Times

NEVER WATCH SAUSAGE – OR DIPLOMACY – BEING MADE.

JIM LARRICK
*Courtesy Columbus
Dispatch*

STANDING SMALL

STUART CARLSON
Courtesy Milwaukee Sentinel

MARK CULLUM
Courtesy Birmingham News

31

JOHN TREVER
Courtesy Albuquerque Journal

"POINDEXTER!"

RAOUL HUNTER
Courtesy Le Soleil (Que.)

JACK HIGGINS
Courtesy Chicago Sun–Times

MIKE SHELTON
*Courtesy Orange County
Register*

ADMIRAL POINDEXTER NAVIGATES UNCHARTED WATERS.

BILL GARNER
Courtesy Washington Times

KIRK WALTERS
Courtesy Toledo Blade

Foreign Affairs

On August 23, Soviet physicist Gennadi Zakharov was arrested on espionage charges in New York. A week later, Nicholas Daniloff, a correspondent for *U.S. News and World Report,* was also arrested in Moscow and accused of spying for the U.S. It was clearly a trumped-up deal by the Soviets, hoping to exchange an American—any American—for Zakharov, who was caught red-handed by the F.B.I. while attempting to buy classified U.S. defense documents.

The Soviets announced that Daniloff would be put on trial, a ploy that outraged Americans. A prisoner exchange was arranged in September and both men were allowed to return to their respective countries.

In October, a cargo plane carrying arms and supplies to the Contras was shot down by the Sandinistas inside Nicaragua. One crewman survived, an American citizen named Eugene Hasenfus, who allegedly had ties to the C.I.A. Hasenfus was tried in Managua and sentenced to 30 years in prison. He was later released when the Ortega government concluded he would be of public relations value in the United States.

Eighteen fighter-bombers based in Britain struck targets in Libya where terrorists were reported to be training. France denied the U.S. use of its air space on the raid, and the attacking pilots were forced to fly a much longer, more hazardous route. One plane was lost, and the French government came in for heavy criticism because of its weak-kneed action.

ADRIAN RAESIDE
Courtesy Times—Colonist (B.C.)

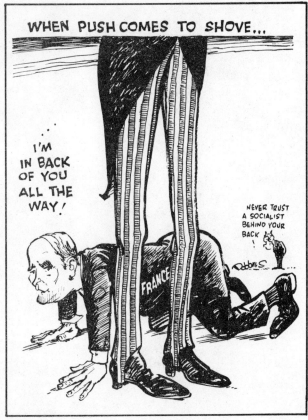

WHEN PUSH COMES TO SHOVE...

I'M IN BACK OF YOU ALL THE WAY!

NEVER TRUST A SOCIALIST BEHIND YOUR BACK!

FRANCE

JIM DOBBINS
Courtesy Union–Leader

AFRICAN NATIONAL CONGRESS

SCOREBOARD

LAND MINES
- 4 CHILDREN/2 ADULTS KILLED
- MANY BLACKS AND WHITES INJURED

BOMBINGS
- 2 CHILDREN/3 ADULTS KILLED

"THE INNOCENT MUST SUFFER FOR THE GREATER GOOD"

JERRY BUCKLEY

JERRY BUCKLEY
Courtesy Montgomery Spirit

NOT IN OUR AIR SPACE YOU DON'T
UNLESS HITLER COMES BACK, OF COURSE

LAFAYETTE, WE WON'T BE THERE.

FRANCE

TO LIBYA →

JACK JURDEN
*Courtesy Wilmington Evening
Journal–News*

CONFERENCE OF NON-ALIGNED NATIONS

PLO
CUBA
LIBYA
NICARAGUA
ZIMBABWE
ANGOLA

BARNETT
THE INDIANAPOLIS NEWS

JERRY BARNETT
Courtesy Indianapolis News

The Iceland Summit

Communist Party General Secretary Mikhail Gorbachev and President Reagan met in October for summit talks in Reykjavik, Iceland but failed to achieve any political breakthroughs. The Russian leader presented several major proposals, including the elimination of Soviet and U.S. medium-range missiles in Europe, a ten-year ban on deployment and testing of anti-missile systems, and a 50 percent reduction in strategic nuclear weapons over a five-year period.

The talks, however, collapsed when Gorbachev also demanded that Reagan dismantle his Strategic Defense Initiative (S.D.I.) program. Reagan remained firm in his refusal to use S.D.I. as a bargaining chip, and the summit meeting went nowhere.

U.S. and Soviet relations as a result remained chilled throughout the rest of 1986. In September, the U.S. ordered the expulsion of 25 members of the Soviet United Nations mission, and a month later the Soviets retaliated by expelling five U.S. diplomats. Two days later, the U.S. ordered 55 more Soviet diplomats to leave the country. Again, the Russians reacted, booting out five more American diplomats and withdrawing the 260 Russian employees at America's embassy in Moscow and consulate in Leningrad.

PAYNE 10-14-86

EUGENE PAYNE
Courtesy Charlotte Observer

MIKE LUCKOVICH
Courtesy New Orleans
Times-Picayune

MIKE GRASTON
Courtesy Windsor Star (Ont.)

"BARTENDER, YET ANOTHER BOTTLE, PLEASE!"

JIM LARRICK
Courtesy Columbus Dispatch

IN ICELAND

EDGAR (SOL) SOLLER
Courtesy California Examiner

WALT HANDELSMAN
Courtesy Scranton Times

ST. GORBACHEV

PAUL SZEP
Courtesy Boston Globe

JERRY FEARING
Courtesy St. Paul Dispatch–Pioneer Press

Elections and Politics

When the ballots in November's elections were tallied, it was apparent that the voters had decided to make sweeping changes. During the pre-election campaign, President Reagan had undertaken a personal campaign to preserve the Republican control of the Senate.

He traveled thousands of miles making speeches and raising money for Republican senatorial contacts, but found that even his great personal popularity could not make the difference at the ballot box this time.

Thus, for the first time since he became president, the Democrats now controlled both houses of Congress, making compromise on Administration programs a way of life during the final two years of his presidency.

In many races across the country mud-slinging seemed to be the standard. The quickie 30-second television commercial proved to be a favorite means for many candidates to make personal attacks on their opponents. In many campaigns, the issues became lost in the mud.

The Rev. Pat Robertson, founder and president of the Christian Broadcasting Network and one of the nation's leading evangelists, announced that he would be a candidate for president in 1988. The liberal opposition immediately cried "foul," even those who enthusiastically had supported the campaigns of religious leaders in the past.

House Speaker Thomas P. O'Neill retired after 34 years in Congress, and Barry Goldwater, the Republican presidential candidate in 1964, announced he would leave the Senate after 33 years.

MIKE LUCKOVICH
Courtesy New Orleans
Times-Picayune

CHARLES WERNER
Courtesy Indianapolis Star

ED GAMBLE
Courtesy Florida Times–Union

BOB JORGENSEN
© Fanfare Editorial Syndicate

PAUL SZEP
Courtesy Boston Globe

GEORGE FISHER
Courtesy Arkansas Gazette

SCOTT WILLIS
Courtesy San Jose Mercury-News

DENNIS RENAULT
Courtesy Sacramento Bee

1986 POLITICAL CAMPAIGN REVIEW

BIG CONTRIBUTORS PARTY LEADERS POLITICAL CONSULTANTS CANDIDATES

'Ac-*cent*-chu-ate the negative/ E-*lim*-inate the positive;
latch *on* to the derogative/ *Don't* mess with Mr. In-Between!'

.. AND THE WINNER IS... (INSERT NAME)

MUD WRESTLING DEMOS '86

JOHN CRAWFORD
Courtesy Alabama Journal

'86 Election Legacy

VOTE FOR

MUD

BOB HOWIE
© Bob Howie Graphics

AREN'T YOU GOING TO VOTE?

I WOULD, BUT I'M A LITTLE UNDER THE LEATHER...

APATHY

J. D. CROWE
*Courtesy Ft. Worth
Star-Telegram*

V. CULLUM ROGERS
Courtesy Durham Morning Herald

JERRY FEARING
Courtesy St. Paul Dispatch–
Pioneer Press

JIMMY MARGULIES
© *Houston Post*

ED STEIN
Courtesy Rocky Mountain News

CLIFF LEVERETTE
© Mississippi Editorial Cartoons

JACK LANIGAN
Courtesy New Bedford
Standard Times

HOUSE SPEAKER TIP O'NEILL

MARK CULLUM
Courtesy Birmingham News

JIM BORGMAN
Courtesy Cincinnati Enquirer

47

DRAPER HILL
Courtesy Detroit News

MARK CULLUM
Courtesy Birmingham News

U.S. Congress

Congress gave President Reagan most of what he asked for in his first two priorities during the year—a federal tax system overhaul and aid to the anti-Sandinista rebels in Nicaragua. Neither victory, however, came easy. The President's defense spending request was cut back and legislators overrode his veto of a bill imposing strong economic and political sanctions against South Africa.

A major part of the Gramm-Rudman balanced-budget law was found to be unconstitutional by the U.S. Supreme Court. Congress had hoped this law would begin to reduce the huge national deficit. Following the ruling, little effort was made to grapple with the problem before congressmen headed home for reelection campaigns.

The tax reform bill was truly revolutionary, wiping out numerous deductions, lowering tax rates, and shifting much of the tax burden from individuals to corporations. It supposedly was to be revenue-neutral, but most Americans seemed resigned to the fact that they would be paying more taxes.

After years of debate, the Senate finally agreed in July to allow permanent television and radio coverage of its proceedings.

Representative Thomas P. O'Neill (D-Mass.), who completed 10 years as speaker of the house—the longest continuous tenure in the history of Congress—announced his retirement.

KEN ALEXANDER
San Francisco Examiner
© Copley News Service

STEVE GREENBERG
*Courtesy Seattle
Post-Intelligencer*

JOHN CRAWFORD
Courtesy Alabama Journal

"I THINK IT HAS SOMETHING TO DO WITH THE GRAMM-RUDMAN ACT."

MILT PRIGGEE
Courtesy Dayton Journal–Herald

"THAT'S RIGHT MR. PRESIDENT...GRAMBO!!"

"What's the commotion about? Our Gramm-Rudman bill was simply a way to put some of our problems on ice"

CHARLES BISSELL
Courtesy The Tennessean

BOB GORRELL
Courtesy Richmond News Leader

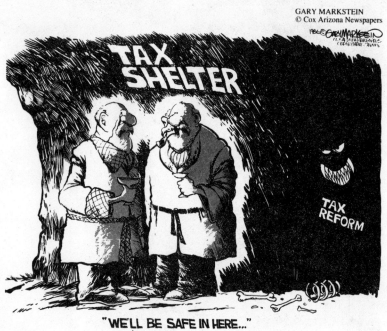

GARY MARKSTEIN
© Cox Arizona Newspapers

"WE'LL BE SAFE IN HERE..."

THE **ONLY** WINNERS UNDER THE TAX REFORM ACT OF 1986:

DOUG REGALIA
Courtesy Contra Costa Sun

i'LL HAVE 80% OF THE LOBSTER SPECIAL.

NEW TAX POLICY

VIC CANTONE
Courtesy New York Daily News

KIRK WALTERS
Courtesy Toledo Blade

ED GAMBLE
Courtesy Florida Times–Union

BRIAN BASSET
Courtesy Seattle Times

SAM RAWLS
Courtesy Atlanta Constitution

WALT HANDELSMAN
Courtesy Scranton Times

DAVID KOLOSTA
Courtesy Houston Post

STEVE SACK
Courtesy Minneapolis Tribune

MIKE KEEFE
Courtesy Denver Post

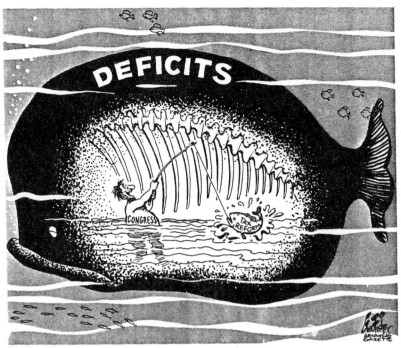

GEORGE FISHER
Courtesy Arkansas Gazette

ART WOOD
Courtesy AFBF (D.C.)

ROBERT DORNFRIED
© Rothco Cartoons

ROBERT DORNFRIED
© Rothco Cartoons

JERRY ROBINSON
© Cartoonists & Writers Syndicate

GEORGE DANBY
Courtesy Bangor Daily News

The Economy

Farm areas and oil-producing states suffered serious economic setbacks in 1986. During the spring and summer, the worst drought and heat wave in over a century battered the southeastern United States, causing an estimated $2.5 billion in losses of crops and livestock. A study released in August concluded that farmers and other workers exposed to herbicides, especially those containing the chemical 2, 4-D for at least twenty days a year, were six times more likely to have lymphatic cancer than those not so exposed.

The outlook for the small farmer failed to improve during the year. Banks continued to foreclose because of farmers' inability to repay loans. Farms that had been in families for generations were being lost as the big farm combines continued to grow.

Oil prices remained low during the year, causing severe repercussions in the oil-producing states. The OPEC countries met in Geneva in August in an attempt to raise oil prices, but to no avail.

Corporation mergers kept executives looking over their shoulders for possible take-over offers, and large banks snapped up failing banks. By mid-year, 62 banks had failed.

Toward the end of 1986 the Big Three automakers found themselves in a heated discount financing battle. General Motors and Ford offered 2.9 percent financing, while Chrysler advertised 2.4 percent. American Motors came up with a zero interest offer.

DRAPER HILL
Courtesy Detroit News

ELDON PLETCHER
© Rothco Cartoons

VIC HARVILLE
Courtesy Texarkana Gazette

CHARLIE DANIEL
Courtesy Knoxville Journal

DANA SUMMERS
Courtesy Orlando Sentinel

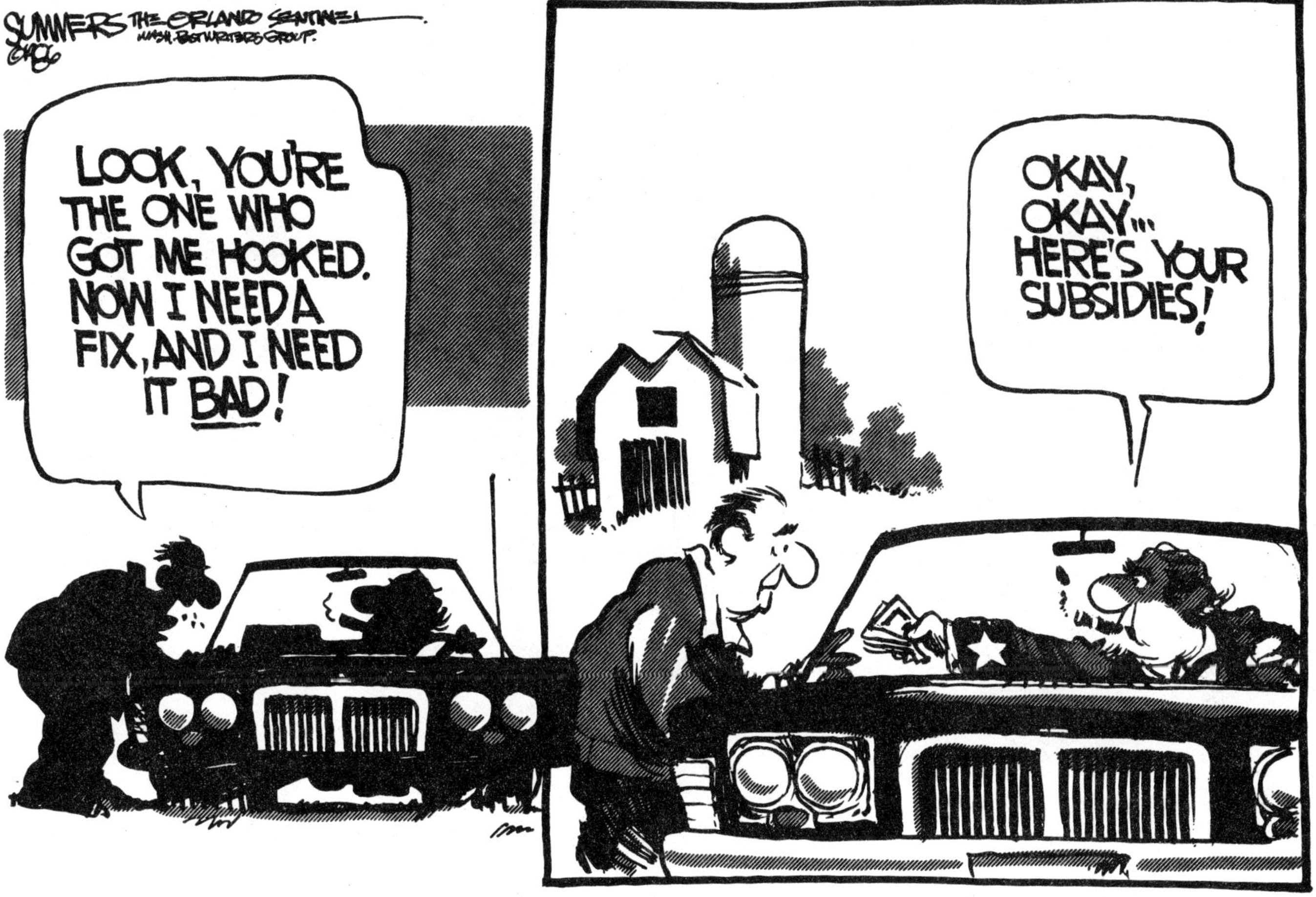
SUMMERS THE ORLANDO SENTINEL WASH. POST WRITERS GROUP
LOOK, YOU'RE THE ONE WHO GOT ME HOOKED. NOW I NEED A FIX, AND I NEED IT BAD!
OKAY, OKAY... HERE'S YOUR SUBSIDIES!

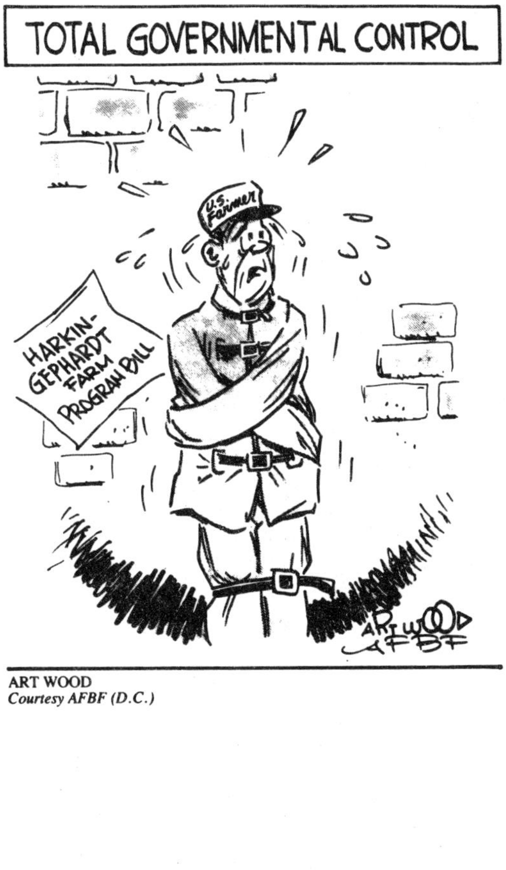
TOTAL GOVERNMENTAL CONTROL
U.S. Farmer
HARKIN-GEPHARDT FARM PROGRAM BILL
ART WOOD AFBF

ART WOOD
Courtesy AFBF (D.C.)

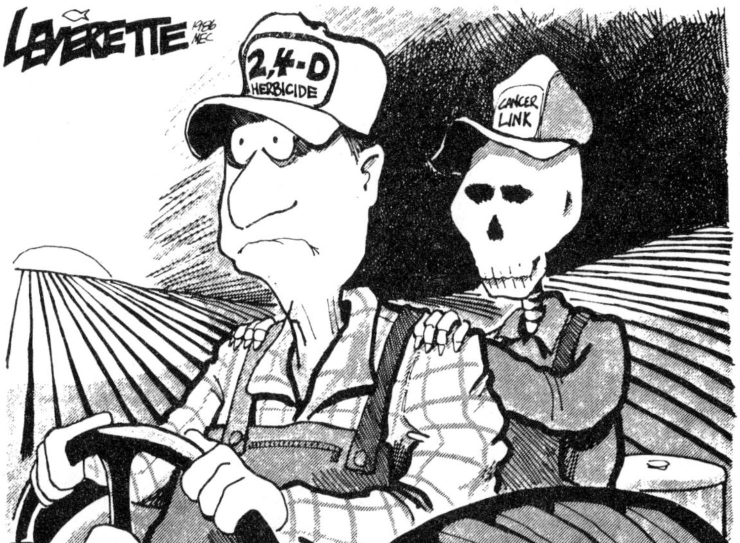
LEVERETTE
2,4-D HERBICIDE
CANCER LINK

CLIFF LEVERETTE
© Mississippi Editorial Cartoons

TOM BECK
© Copley News Service

BOB JORGENSEN
© Fanfare Editorial Syndicate

"Left-Wing Terrorists?" "No, Insider Trading"

TOM FLANNERY
Courtesy Baltimore Sun

BOB GORRELL
Courtesy Richmond News Leader

63

STEVE HILL
Courtesy Oklahoma Gazette

JEFF KOTERBA
Courtesy Bellevue (Neb.) Leader

JIM LANGE
Courtesy Daily Oklahoman

STEVE TURTIL
© Rothco

BUBBA FLINT
Courtesy Arlington (Tex.) Daily

MARTIN E. GARRITY
Courtesy Fair Oaks Post (Calif.)

Central America

The U.S. House of Representatives voted in June to restore military aid to the Contras, and the leftist Sandinista government clamped down even harder on civil liberties in Nicaragua. President Daniel Ortega ordered the opposition newspaper *La Prensa* to cease publication. Bishop Pablo Antonio Vega was expelled from the country for allegedly lobbying for Contra aid in the U.S., and Rev. Bismarck Carballo was not allowed to return to Nicaragua from a trip abroad because of his anti-Sandinista stand.

The fortunes of the Contras sagged during the first half of the year, but the prospects for renewed aid spurred rebel leaders to launch new offensives. The Sandinistas, however, had greatly increased their fleet of Russian transport and armored helicopters, vital in jungle warfare.

In June, the International Court of Justice, or World Court, ordered the U.S. to stop arming and training rebels and to pay reparations to Nicaragua. The U.S., however, refused to recognize the court's authority.

A cargo plane laden with supplies for the Contras was shot down in Nicaragua and an American crewman, Eugene Hasenfus, was captured. He told his captors he thought he was working for the C.I.A. He was convicted by a "people tribunal," sentenced to 30 years, and then released.

Mexico's economic situation continued to deteriorate during the year, and the government's political problems increased. Reagan met twice with the Mexican president and helped float a $12 billion loan to the beleaguered country.

ED GAMBLE
Courtesy Florida Times–Union

EUGENE PAYNE
Courtesy Charlotte Observer

BRIAN GABLE
Courtesy Regina Leader–Post (Sask.)

'I've never seen it before!'

69

TOM FLANNERY
Courtesy Baltimore Sun

Lest We Forget

KEN ALEXANDER
San Francisco Examiner
© Copley News Service

National Defense

The Reagan Administration announced in May that it would no longer abide by the unratified Strategic Arms Limitation Treaty of 1979 (Salt II), charging that the Soviets had repeatedly violated the agreement. The limitation of arms was discussed at the Iceland Summit, but no real progress was made after Gorbachev insisted that restrictions be imposed on the President's Star Wars program.

Congress ratified legislation that gave the Pentagon $290 billion for fiscal 1987—$30 billion below the funding Reagan had sought. The President's S.D.I. program was cut back sharply as a result, and other defense requests were reduced. In spite of the cutback for fiscal 1987, S.D.I. research actually accelerated during 1986, and several successful tests were reported in the long-range program.

An $11 billion battlefield air-defense system was approved by the Pentagon in August. The new program, called Forward Area Air Defense, would involve carrying heavy missiles on armored chassis and lighter missiles on trucks. These would replace the Sergeant York anti-aircraft gun program that was canceled in 1985 after tests proved it to be ineffective.

RAY OSRIN
Courtesy Cleveland Plain Dealer

ROY PETERSON
Courtesy Vancouver Sun

CHARLES BISSELL
Courtesy The Tennessean

- AFTER A NUCLEAR HOLOCAUST -

MIKE ANGELO
Courtesy Main Line Times

'Just Give Me My Turn — That's All I Ask'

TOM ENGELHARDT
Courtesy St. Louis Post–Dispatch

JOSEPH SZABO
© Rothco

JOHN KNUDSEN
Courtesy L.A. Tidings

WELL, WILL YOU SELL IT FOR TEN MILLION?

U.S. Army spends 600 million on a drone airplane that still doesn't work (News item)

"but if the salt has lost its flavor it is then good for nothing but to be thrown out and trampled under foot by men..."
—Matthew 5:13

SALT II

NO! NEIN! NON! NO!

NATO ALLIES

RR

© 1986 NY FILIPINO REPORTE

DANI AGUILA
Courtesy Filipino Reporter

PITTSBURGH PRESS 86

REACH, RUSSKIE SPY!!...

UN

ROB ROGERS
Courtesy Pittsburgh Press

Crime and the Courts

Chief Justice Warren E. Burger announced in June that he would retire at the end of the 1986 term, a move that many saw as the beginning of a new era on the U.S. Supreme Court. To fill the vacancy, President Reagan turned to perhaps the most conservative member of the court, elevating William H. Rehnquist to chief justice. He also appointed another conservative, Antonin Scalia, as associate justice. Rehnquist's appointment provoked a flood of protests from a wide array of Democrats and liberal Republicans who questioned his commitment to civil liberties and civil rights.

In a controversial privacy case, the court ruled that there is no constitutional right to engage in homosexual relations. The court also ruled in favor of the government's right to use technological means to detect wrongdoing.

One of the year's biggest news stories was the continuing fight to halt drug trafficking. Crack, a potent and highly addictive form of cocaine, increased in popularity, and police in New York City blamed its use for an 18 percent jump in robberies.

The rapid rise in liability insurance rates moved many doctors to cease practicing certain types of medicine, and the development of new products slowed dramatically, especially in the pharmaceutical industry.

Attorney General Edwin Meese issued a report on pornography which held that pornography depicting violent sex can lead to sexual violence.

MIKE PETERS
Courtesy Dayton Daily News

WAIT...I THINK WE'D BETTER HAVE OUR LAWYER PRESENT.

JOHN BRANCH
Courtesy San Antonio Express–News

BRUCE BEATTIE
*Courtesy Daytona Beach
News–Journal*

"We've got another product tampering case on our hands... they tried executing me with cyanide, but only my headache went away."

CHAIRS

ONCE UPON A TIME ~...

DEATH ROW

TODAY !-

DEATH ROW

The Daily Oklahoman

LANGE

JIM LANGE
Courtesy Daily Oklahoman

Berry's World

© 1986 by NEA, Inc.   Jim Berry

"Chief Justice Burger urges fines for frivolous suits and that's about as FRIVOLOUS a suit as I've ever seen."

JIM BERRY
© NEA

GARY BROOKINS
Courtesy Richmond Times–Dispatch

"YOUR SCHEDULE HERE WILL BE EXERCISE PERIOD AT 10:00, LUNCH AT NOON AND YOUR FIRST PAROLE HEARING AT 2:00...."

" THIS IS MY LAWYER... IN CASE YOU DO ANYTHING ILLEGAL ! "

"Are we looking for something for birds, animals or people?"

JOHN DEERING
Courtesy Arkansas Democrat

MIKE PETERS
Courtesy Dayton Daily News

"--AND SO WE RETURNED TO THE CAVES BECAUSE WE COULDN'T AFFORD THE LIABILITY INSURANCE"

ART HENRIKSON
Courtesy Arlington Hts.
Daily Herald

"THE TREE DONE IT!"

EUGENE PAYNE
Courtesy Charlotte Observer

BOB ENGLEHART
Courtesy Hartford Courant

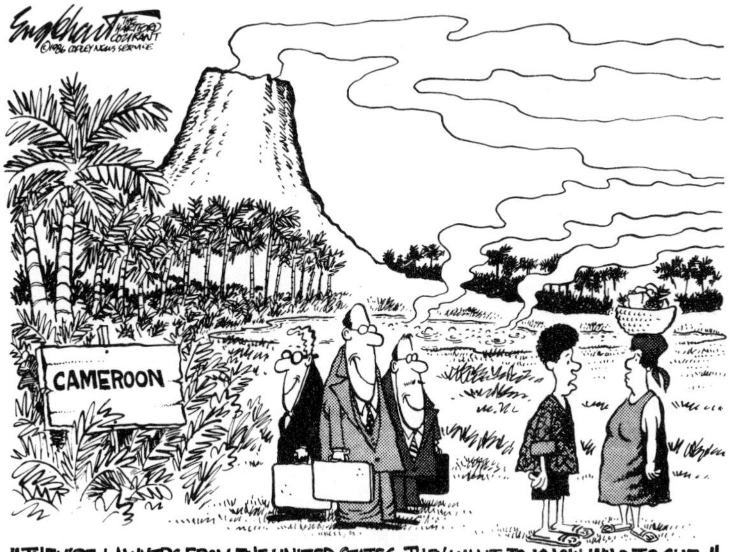
CAMEROON

"THEY'RE LAWYERS FROM THE UNITED STATES. THEY WANT TO KNOW WHO TO SUE."

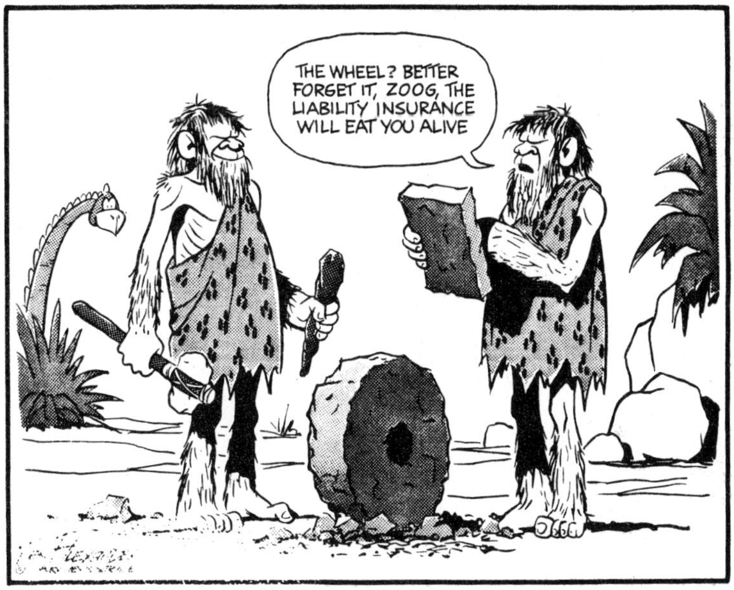
THE WHEEL? BETTER FORGET IT, ZOOG, THE LIABILITY INSURANCE WILL EAT YOU ALIVE

KEN ALEXANDER
San Francisco Examiner
© Copley News Service

GARY BROOKINS
Courtesy Richmond Times–Dispatch

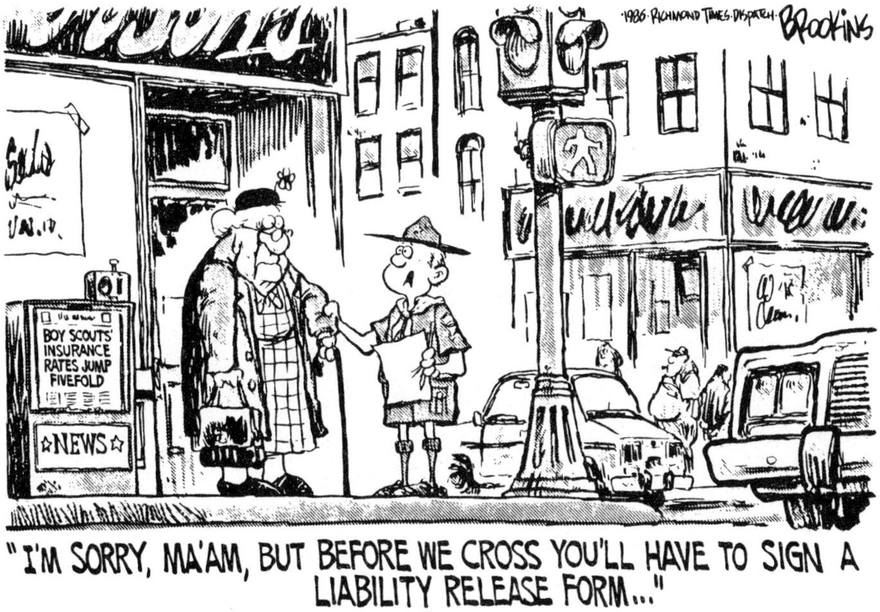
©1986 · RICHMOND TIMES-DISPATCH · BROOKINS
BOY SCOUTS' INSURANCE RATES JUMP FIVEFOLD
NEWS

"I'M SORRY, MA'AM, BUT BEFORE WE CROSS YOU'LL HAVE TO SIGN A LIABILITY RELEASE FORM..."

DOC GOODWIN
Courtesy Columbus (O.) Dispatch

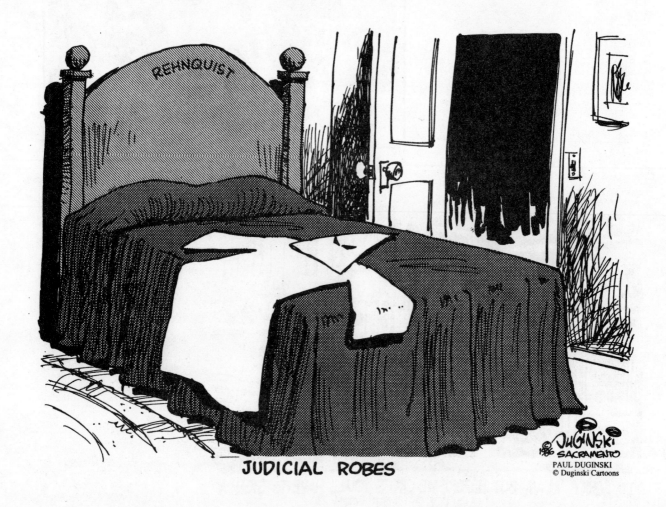

JUDICIAL ROBES

PAUL DUGINSKI
© Duginski Cartoons

82

BOB ENGLEHART
Courtesy Hartford Courant

JIM LARRICK
Courtesy Columbus Dispatch

"THE CONFIRMATION IS COMPLETE. LET BYGONES BE BYGONES."

"Harder to Starboard, Aye-Aye-, Sir - I'll Try!"

TOM FLANNERY
Courtesy Baltimore Sun

DAN WASSERMAN
Courtesy Boston Globe

FIRST THE GOOD NEWS . . .

ELDON PLETCHER
© Rothco Cartoons

The Mideast

In late 1985, attacks by Palestinian terrorists at airports in Vienna and Rome left several Americans dead and injured. As 1986 began, U.S. Naval vessels and aircraft clashed with Libyan forces in the Gulf of Sidra, off the Libyan coast. Then, in April, a West Berlin nightclub was bombed by terrorists, killing two U.S. servicemen.

President Reagan, who accused Libyan leader Moammar Qaddafi of aiding the Berlin attackers and of being involved in earlier bombings, promised retaliation if the heinous acts continued. Ten days after the nightclub bombing, American warplanes based in Great Britain and on carriers in the Mediterranean attacked targets in Libya where terrorists were being trained. Qaddafi's residence was hit and his adopted daughter reportedly was killed.

The planes from Britain were forced to fly several thousand miles further to reach their targets when France refused to allow overflights. All the planes but one returned safely.

For months before the strike, Qaddafi regularly denounced the U.S., but turned silent and went into hiding for months after the raid.

The plunge in world oil prices continued as the oil glut remained, despite efforts to cut back production by the **OPEC** nations. The excess of oil seemed to be hurting **OPEC** more than it was hurting non-**OPEC** producers in the North Sea.

EDD ULUSCHAK
Courtesy Edmonton Journal

PHIL BISSELL
Courtesy Lowell (Mass.) Sun

JOHN STAMPONE
Courtesy Suncoast News

STEVE MCBRIDE
Courtesy Independence (Kan.)
Daily Reporter

PETER B. WALLACE
Courtesy Boston Herald

JON KENNEDY
Courtesy Arkansas Democrat

SAM RAWLS
Courtesy Atlanta Constitution

88

DOUG MACGREGOR
Courtesy Norwich Bulletin

JIM PALMER
Courtesy Montgomery Advertiser

PAUL SZEP
Courtesy Boston Globe

89

DAN WASSERMAN
Courtesy Boston Globe

EDD ULUSCHAK
Courtesy Edmonton Journal

90

"WITH THE COLLAPSE OF THE OPEC TALKS THERE SEEMS TO BE NO END TO THE UNDERCUTTING OF THE PRICE OF OIL ..."

MILT PRIGGEE
Courtesy Dayton Journal–Herald

JOHN BRANCH
Courtesy San Antonio Express–News

JIM DOBBINS
Courtesy Union–Leader

TOM ENGELHARDT
Courtesy St. Louis Post–Dispatch

BOB RICH
Courtesy New Haven Register

The Philippines

"People power" in the Philippines overthrew the entrenched and corrupt regime of President Ferdinand E. Marcos in 1986 after 20 years of almost absolute power. A demure former housewife, Corazon Aquino, became president of the republic, a genuine political phenomenon.

The Philippine citizenry had become disillusioned with Marcos and his wife Imelda, who together had amassed great wealth and personal power as the country's economy sagged lower and lower. Seething opposition to the Marcos regime had broken out in 1983 when Aquino's husband, Benigno Aquino, a leading opposition figure, was assassinated at Manila Airport. When opposition to Marcos finally began to gather strength, the president called an election for February, apparently thinking he still could win reelection handily. His operatives allegedly stole ballot boxes, rigged vote counts, and even shot Aquino supporters. By the official count, which he controlled, Marcos said he won. But a citizen's group concluded otherwise, and the country teetered on the brink of civil war.

Marcos, with the help of the U.S., fled to Hawaii after the military divided its loyalty and crowds converged on the presidential palace. Aquino appointed a commission to seek recovery of several billion dollars Marcos allegedly looted from the country's treasury. At year's end, Aquino maintained a broad base of popular support.

JIM BORGMAN
Courtesy Cincinnati Enquirer

93

ED STEIN
Courtesy Rocky Mountain News

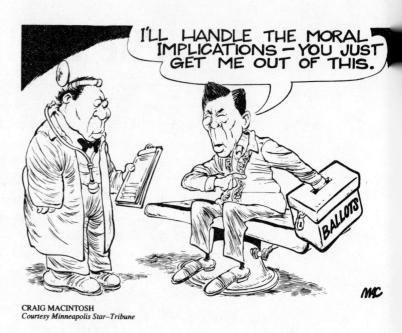

CRAIG MACINTOSH
Courtesy Minneapolis Star–Tribune

DARCY
Newsday cartoon by Tom Darcy

'The people are behind me.' — Pres. Marcos, February 16, 1986

TOM DARCY
Courtesy Newsday

'Now, That Structure Over There Is Our Famous Washington Monument'

CHARLES WERNER
Courtesy Indianapolis Star

"I DON'T KNOW WHAT I MISS MORE, IMELDA...
LOOTING PUBLIC FUNDS OR HAVING PEOPLE SHOT!"

DAVID HORSEY
Courtesy Seattle Post-Intelligencer

WHEN YOU ABSOLUTELY, POSITIVELY, HAVE TO GET OUT OVERNIGHT...

TYRANNICAL EXPRESS

JIMMY MARGULIES
© Houston Post

MARGULIES
©1986 HOUSTON POST

BOB GORRELL
Courtesy Richmond News Leader

MANILA VICE

EDGAR (SOL) SOLLER
Courtesy California Examiner

SOMEONE BROKE INTO THE PALACE AND STOLE NEXT MONTH'S ELECTION RESULTS

MARCOS

EDD ULUSCHAK
Courtesy Edmonton Journal

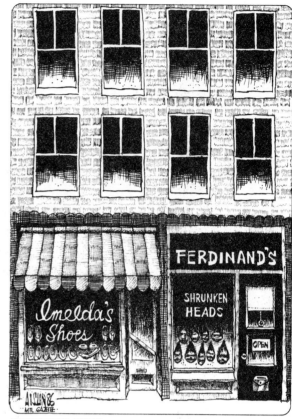

FERDINAND'S

SHRUNKEN HEADS

Imelda's Shoes

OPEN

TERRY MOSHER (AISLIN)
Courtesy Montreal Gazette

ANYTHING TO DECLARE?

U.S. CUSTOMS

DICK LOCHER
Courtesy Chicago Tribune

97

JOHN TREVER
Courtesy Albuquerque Journal

MIKE LUCKOVICH
*Courtesy New Orleans
Times-Picayune*

The Soviet Union

The bloody stalemate in Afghanistan continued apace as the Soviets relentlessly pursued their objective of crushing all resistance to the Moscow-dominated Marxist government in Kabul. It was estimated that more than one-half of the Afghan population had been driven from their homes since the war began. Although the Soviets maintained a force of some 115,000 troops and enjoyed a vast superiority in equipment and firepower, the Afghans valiantly fought on.

The worst nuclear power accident in history rocked the Soviet Union in April at the town of Chernobyl in the Ukraine. An unauthorized test was being conducted, and one of the reactors involved went out of control with a sudden burst of power. Two explosions followed, setting numerous fires and spewing large amounts of radioactivity into the atmosphere. True to form, the Soviet government had little to report about the accident until a frightened world demanded information.

As far as is known, at least 31 people died in the explosion and aftermath, and well over 100,000 residents of the surrounding area were evacuated, many perhaps permanently. Large tracts of agricultural land were made unusable because of fallout, and experts forecast that many more thousands of Russians would die from radioactivity during the coming years. The tragedy forced other industrialized nations to examine anew their nuclear power policies.

DICK LOCHER
Courtesy Chicago Tribune

VIC CANTONE
© Rothco

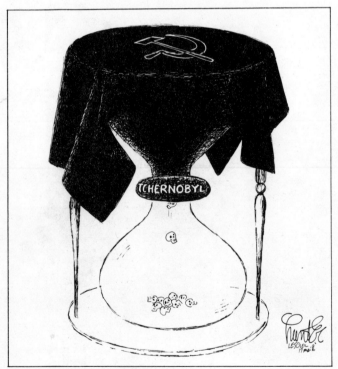

RAOUL HUNTER
Courtesy Le Soleil (Que.)

DICK GIBSON
Courtesy Toronto Sun

ROY PETERSON
Courtesy Vancouver Sun

JOE HELLER
Courtesy Green Bay Press-Gazette

RANDY WICKS
Courtesy Newhall (Calif.) Signal

"SURE, THAT NUKE ACCIDENT WAS SERIOUS — ALMOST SPOILED POLAND'S MILK AN' THE SOVIETS' VODKA!"

BRUCE BEATTIE
Courtesy Daytona Beach News–Journal

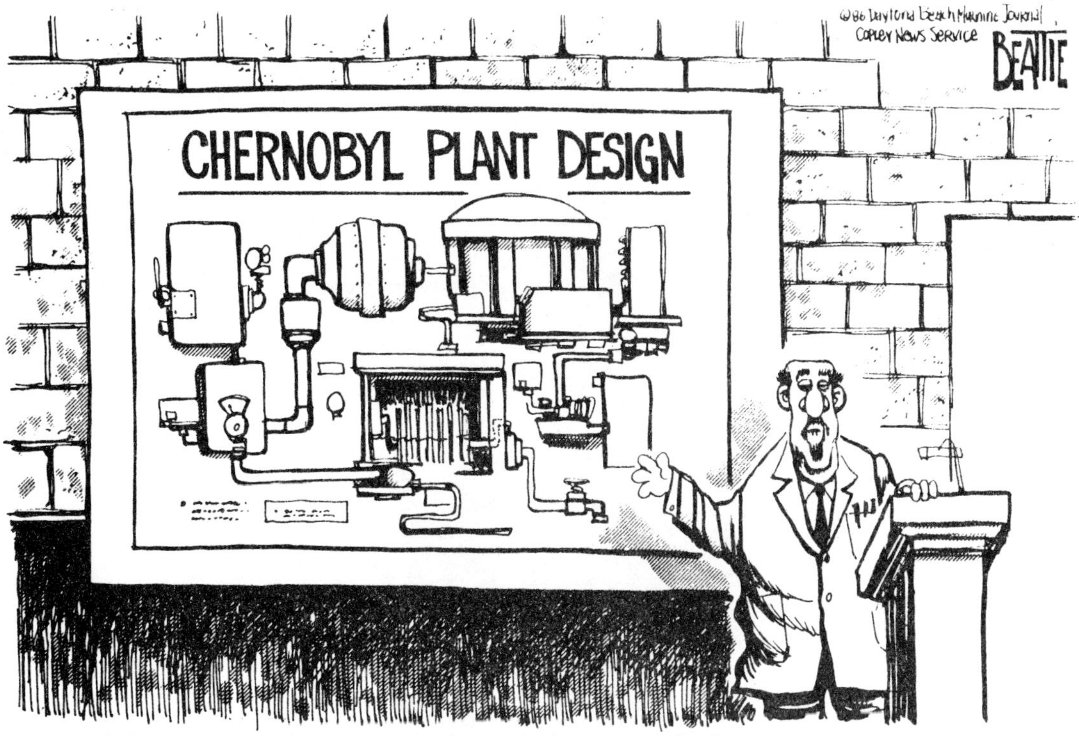
BEATTIE
CHERNOBYL PLANT DESIGN

"Of course we have a containment structure... is designed to keep NEWS from being released!"

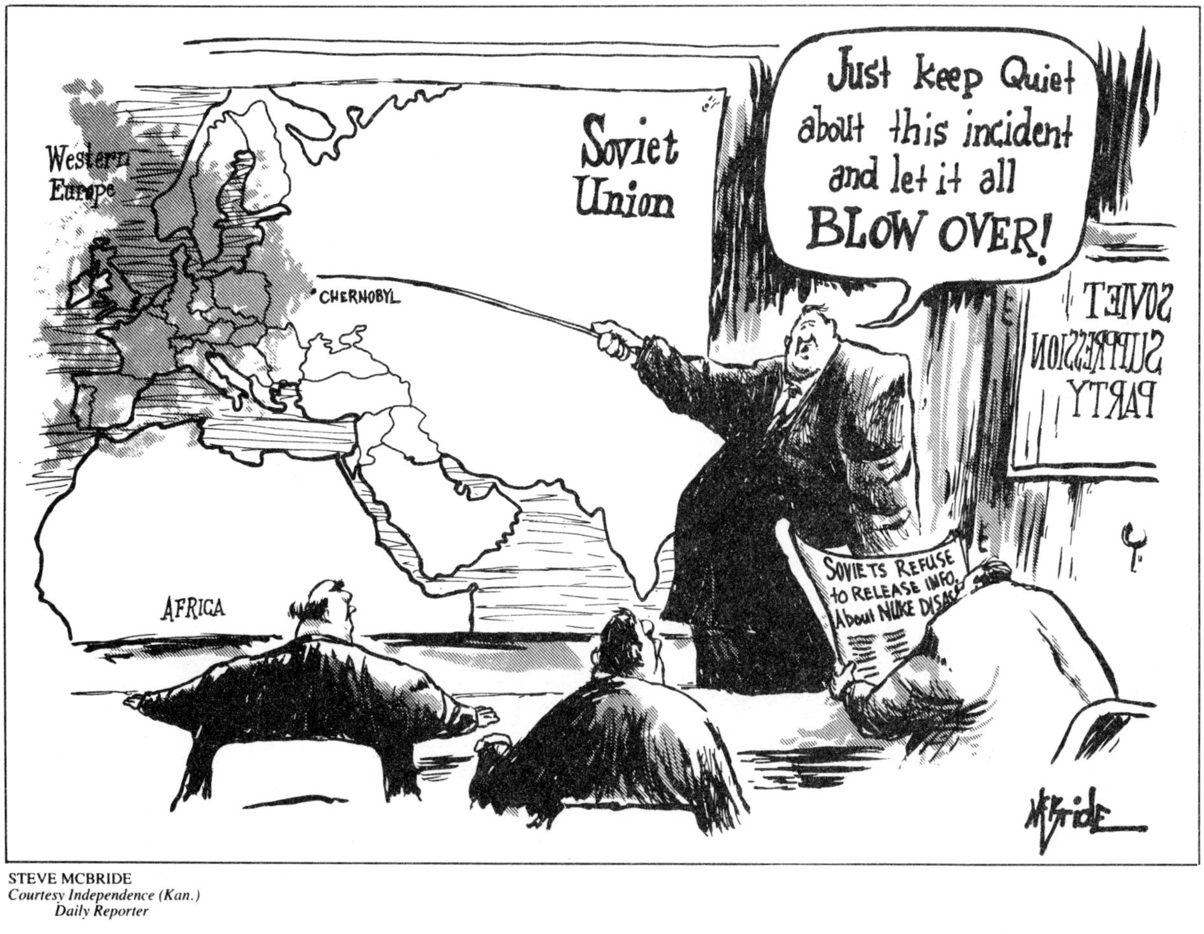
Just keep Quiet about this incident and let it all BLOW OVER!
Soviet Union
Western Europe
CHERNOBYL
AFRICA
SOVIET SUPPRESSION PARTY
SOVIETS REFUSE to RELEASE INFO. About NUKE DISA
McBRIDE

STEVE MCBRIDE
Courtesy Independence (Kan.) Daily Reporter

HY ROSEN
Courtesy Albany Times–Union

LAMBERT DER
Courtesy Greenville News-Piedmont

THE DANILOFF MANEUVER

RAY OSRIN
Courtesy Cleveland Plain Dealer

TOM ADDISON
Courtesy The Journal (S.C.)

CHUCK AYERS
Courtesy Akron Beacon–Journal

DANA SUMMERS
Courtesy Orlando Sentinel

JERRY BYRD
Courtesy Beaumont Enterprise

South Africa

Confrontation and violence frequently descended upon black areas of explosive South Africa during the year. Many of the attacks were staged by black vigilante groups against other blacks accused of collaborating with the Pretoria government. The vigilantes often were encouraged and sometimes were paid to act, according the the Rev. Allan Boesak, a leader for the black United Democratic Front.

Organized rent strikes were staged in communities across the nation. Local government authorities depend on such rents as a major source of income. In August, more than 20 people were killed in an incident in which renters, fearing eviction, had barricaded the streets. The deaths occurred when violence flared as authorities attempted to clear the streets.

President P. W. Botha declared in June that a state of emergency had been imposed to curb violence by the outlawed African National Congress, the black nationalist group attempting to oust the Pretoria government. During the emergency, security forces were given wide-ranging powers, including the right to conduct searches without warrants and the authority to halt any political activity.

During the year, an increasingly hostile Congress voted strong economic sanctions against South Africa. Reagan vetoed the measure, but the veto was overridden.

DAVID CATROW
Courtesy Springfield (O.)
News-Sun

"Our accountants have just informed us that divesting from South Africa is the only moral and ethical thing to do."

'We Won't Negotiate With The ANC Because
It Is A Terrorist Organization'

SAM RAWLS
Courtesy Atlanta Constitution

MIKE PETERS
Courtesy Dayton Daily News

'Stand firm here? Mr. Botha, are you sure you grasp the gravity of the situation?'

TOM DARCY
Courtesy Newsday

The making of tomorrow's terrorist?

TOM FLOYD
Courtesy Gary Post-Tribune

H. CLAY BENNETT
Courtesy St. Petersburg Times

DICK LOCHER
Courtesy Chicago Tribune

JOHN TREVER
Courtesy Albuquerque Journal

"SHEESH! WHEN'S HE GONNA SHOW SOME LEADERSHIP AND FALL IN LINE??"

JERRY ROBINSON
© Cartoonists & Writers Syndicate

BOB TAYLOR
Courtesy Dallas Times–Herald

112

Space

After 55 successful manned space flights in 25 years without an inflight fatality, NASA's safety record was broken on January 28, 1986. The space shuttle Challenger exploded shortly after liftoff, and its seven crew members perished. The flight had been delayed several times, but launch finally was made at 11:38 a.m. The temperature had dropped to a freezing 28 degrees during the night, but had risen to 36 degrees by liftoff.

Just 73 seconds after launching, television viewers across the nation watched in horror as balls of fire filled the Florida sky. Dead were flight commander Francis Scobee, pilot Michael J. Smith, mission specialists Ellison Onizuka, Judith Resnik, and Ronald McNair, Hughes Aircraft engineer Gregory Jarvis, and schoolteacher Christa McAuliffe. McAuliffe, a high school social studies teacher from New Hampshire, had won a national competition for a berth on the flight. She was to have given the children of the world their first lessons from space.

A special commision conducted a lengthy investigation of the fatal flight and released its findings in June. The report called for widespread reforms in NASA's operations and strongly recommended redesign of the faulty joint and O-ring seal, which were found to be the primary causes of the disaster.

GEORGE FISHER
Courtesy Arkansas Gazette

DICK WALLMEYER
Courtesy Independent Press–Telegram
(Calif.)

JACK MCLEOD
© Army Times

114

DANA SUMMERS
Courtesy Orlando Sentinel

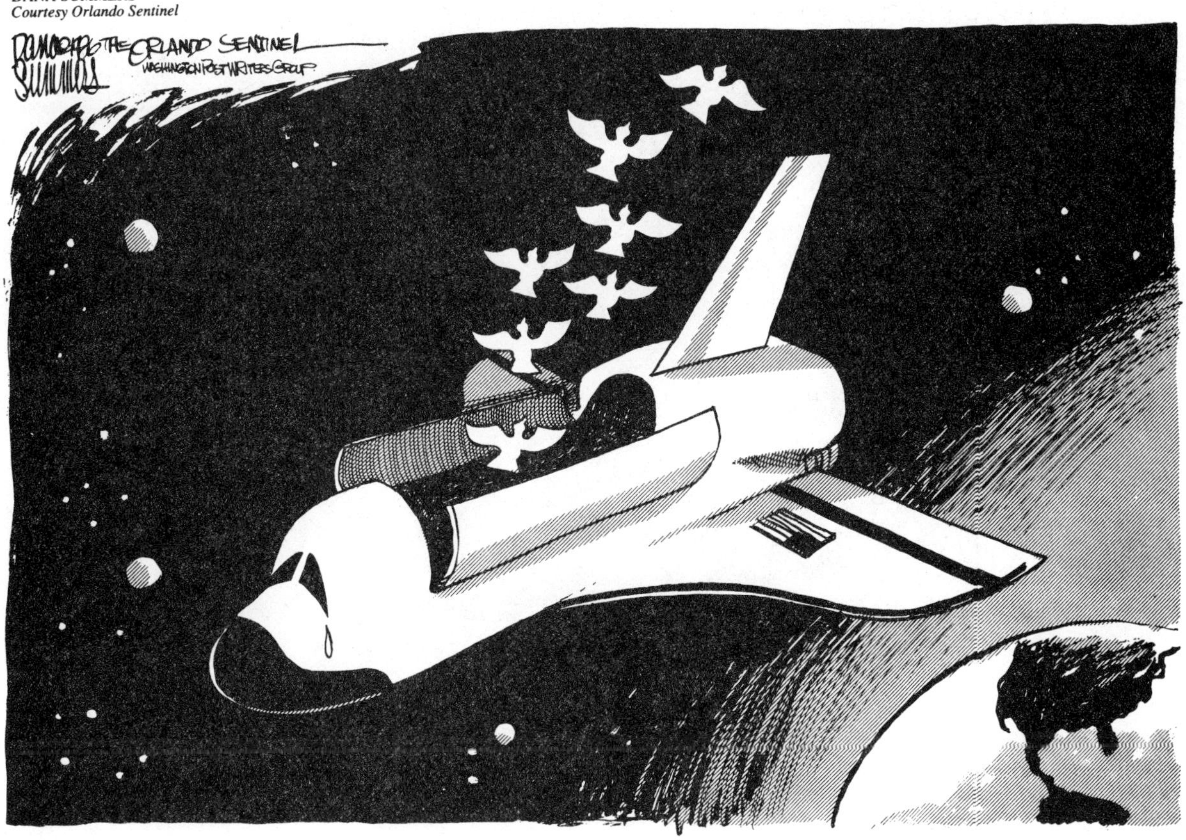
DANA SUMMERS THE ORLANDO SENTINEL
WASHINGTON POST WRITERS GROUP

MIKE SHELTON
Courtesy Orange County Register

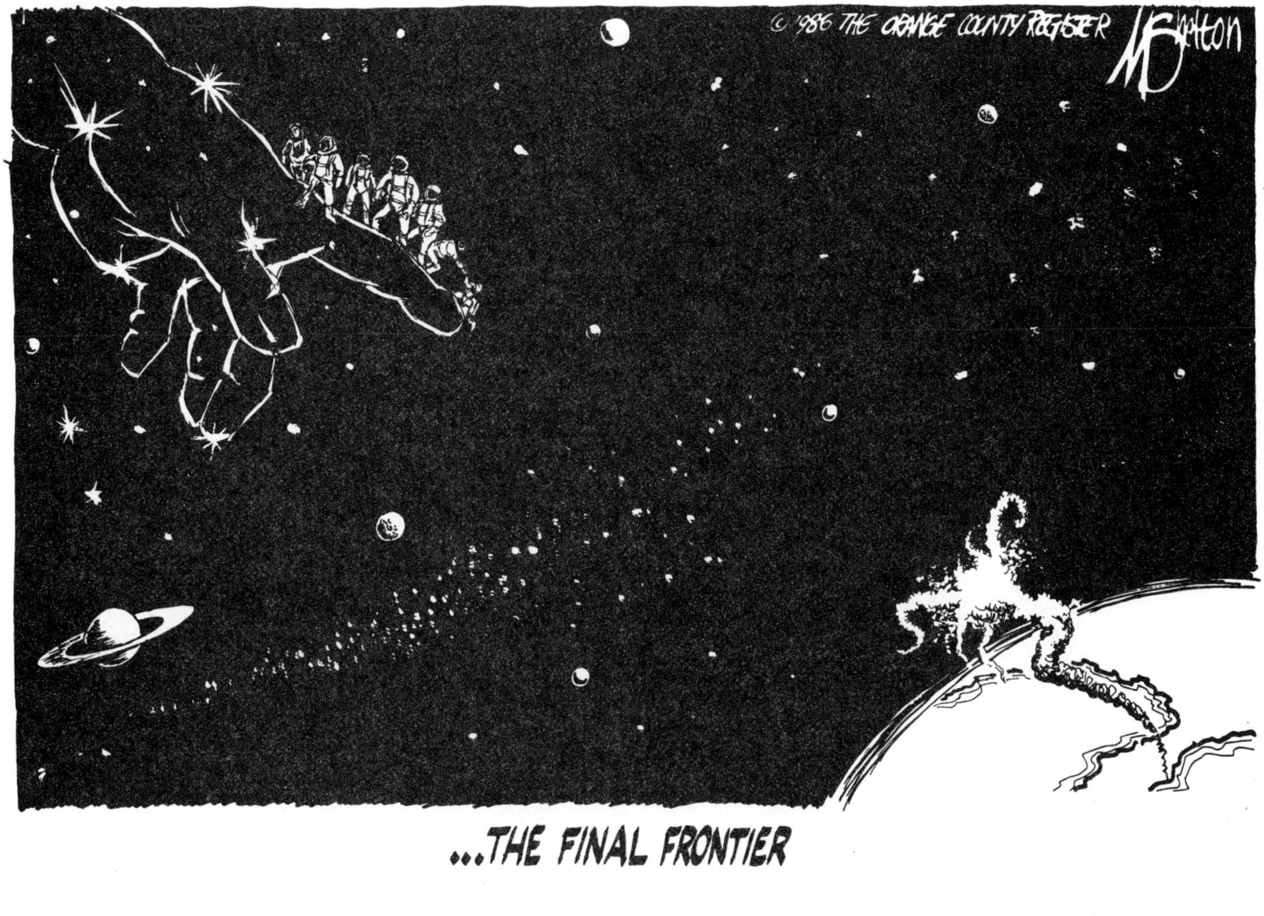
© 1986 THE ORANGE COUNTY REGISTER
MShelton
...THE FINAL FRONTIER

DAVID KOLOSTA
Courtesy Houston Post

MARTIN E. GARRITY
Courtesy Fair Oaks Post (Calif.)

JOHN MILT MORRIS
© Associated Press

RE THINK

NASA

Berry's World

NASA

"...and another thing — FIX THAT SIGN."

NASA

CHALLENGER DISASTER

CHUCK AYERS
Courtesy Akron Beacon–Journal

JERRY BARNETT
Courtesy Indianapolis News

JERRY FEARING
Courtesy St. Paul Dispatch–
Pioneer Press

SDI (Star Wars)

Debate swirled around President Reagan's ambitious and costly Strategic Defense Initiative (Star Wars) program throughout the year. Critics expressed grave doubts about the feasibility of the project and claimed it would be far too expensive. Congress was unwilling to fund all the testing and research for the project that the Administration had sought. The largest budget item for the Defense Department was a $4.8 billion request for S.D.I., but this was trimmed by Congress to $3.5 billion.

S.D.I. research accelerated during 1986, and the Pentagon reported that several tests had shown the technological feasibility of the program. The U.S. signed agreements with Great Britain, West Germany, Italy, and Israel which permit their participation in S.D.I. research and and development. Negotiations were also underway for Japan to be included as well.

At the October summit in Iceland, President Reagan was unwilling to bargain away S.D.I. in exchange for sizeable cutbacks in American and Soviet nuclear arsenals.

GARY BROOKINS
Courtesy Richmond Times–Dispatch

"YOUR SHIELD, SIRE !"

LAZARO FRESQUET
Courtesy El Miami Herald

LINDA BOILEAU
Courtesy Frankfort State Journal

TOM FLANNERY
Courtesy Baltimore Sun

"Don't Embarrass Me--PRETEND You Understand It"

JERRY ROBINSON
© Cartoonists & Writers Syndicate

BILL MITCHELL
Courtesy Potomac News

Air Travel

Terrorism continued to plague the world's airlines during 1986. In April, a bomb exploded on a TWA jet flying from Rome to Athens, killing four passengers. Then, in May, 16 people died in Sri Lanka when a bomb rocked a plane while passengers were boarding. The attempted hijacking of a Pan American jumbo jet at Karachi Airport in Pakistan resulted in the deaths of 21 people in September. As a result, security measures were beefed up even more at airports around the world.

Mid-air collisions and near-collisions continued to increase. Often small private aircraft were involved. In October, a small Piper plane collided with a Mexican DC-9 near Los Angeles International Airport, killing all 67 people aboard the planes and 15 people on the ground.

The U.S. airline industry was marked by mergers and acquisitions during the year. Northwest purchased Republic for $884 million, while TWA bought Ozark for some $250 million, and Delta and Western announced an $860 million merger deal. Eastern merged with Texas Air, making Texas Air the largest airline operation in the U.S. In September, Texas Air also announced plans to acquire People Express for $116 million. People Express, one of the first bargain-rate airlines, had experienced financial difficulty because of a too-fast rate of growth and increased competition from other rate-cutters.

WAYNE STAYSKAL
Courtesy Tampa Tribune

" YOU WANT TO KNOW THE AIR FARE FROM TAMPA TO WASHINGTON?... JUST A MINUTE, PLEASE! "

STEVE SACK
Courtesy Minneapolis Tribune

AL LIEDERMAN
© Rothco

MERLE TINGLEY
Courtesy London Free Press (Can.)

BOB ENGLEHART
Courtesy Hartford Courant

WAYNE STAYSKAL
Courtesy Tampa Tribune

Statue of Liberty

America's famous Lady was the center of attraction on Fourth of July weekend when thousands of people in New York Harbor, along with millions across the nation, celebrated her complete renovation. A mammoth restoration of Miss Liberty had begun in 1983, with Chrysler Corporation President Lee Iacocca leading a group to raise funds for the project. Of the $277 million collected, some $70 million was spent to restore the statue. The remainder will be used to develop and refurbish Ellis Island.

In a nationally televised ceremony on July 3, the new copper torch held by Miss Liberty was rekindled by President Reagan. An armada of tall ships was on hand, and the sky blazed with fireworks.

In the restoration, the interior of the statue was completely cleaned, a weak shoulder joint was strengthened, and all corroded parts were replaced. And the renovated pedestal now offers a hydraulic glass-walled elevator.

MIKE LUCKOVICH
Courtesy New Orleans
Times-Picayune

HER CROWNING GLORY

EDDIE GERMANO
Courtesy Brockton Daily Enterprise

ED GAMBLE
Courtesy Florida Times–Union

RAY OSRIN
Courtesy Cleveland Plain Dealer

126

Canada

Opening free-trade with the U.S. ranked as the most controversial issue in Canada during 1986. Prime Minister Brian Mulroney's decision to pursue a free-trade agreement with the neighbor to the south inspired a vigorous public debate. Canada is the largest single trading partner of the U.S., accounting for nearly $170 million in 1985. But when the U.S. slapped a 35 percent tariff on Canadian cedar shakes and shingles, Mulroney quickly retaliated by adding new tariffs on U.S. goods. In October, the U.S. acted again, imposing a 15 percent import duty on Canadian softwood lumber, and Canada again reacted with a duty on U.S. corn.

Much of the opposition to Mulroney's free-trade policy was generated by those who felt Canada would lose not only jobs but cultural, social, and regional development programs as well. A series of conflict-of-interest scandals within the government caused Mulroney to lose favor with many voters, but he took quick action by rearranging his cabinet and reorganizing the senior bureaucracy.

Acid rain remained an issue, and Canada pressed the U.S. to spend $5 billion on a program to reduce emissions from factories in the U.S.

MERLE TINGLEY
Courtesy London Free Press (Can.)

"WELLL, BRIAN, YOU COULD BE RIGHT ... IT MAY BE RAINING ... BUT, THEN AGAIN ...!"

MERLE TINGLEY
Courtesy London Free Press (Can.)

ANDY DONATO
Courtesy Toronto Sun

JOSH BEUTEL
Courtesy Saint John
Telegraph–Journal

ADRIAN RAESIDE
Courtesy Times–Colonist (B.C.)

ANDY DONATO
Courtesy Toronto Sun

TERRY MOSHER (AISLIN)
Courtesy Montreal Gazette

129

Sports and Drugs

The United States Football League died in 1986 when the $1.69 billion antitrust suit filed against the NFL was settled. It was a curious verdict. A U.S. district court jury found the NFL guilty of violating antitrust laws, but awarded the USFL only one dollar in compensation. The verdict was appealed, but to no avail. In August, the struggling new league released all its players from their contracts, allowing them to seek jobs with NFL teams.

Drug problems seemed to envelope sports during the year. A basketball star, Len Bias, died of cocaine poisoning just two days after being selected in the first round of the NBA draft by the Boston Celtics. Don Rogers, a standout safety for the Cleveland Browns football team, also died of cocaine poisoning. Many other athletes, professional and amateur, were found to be using drugs. Some were convicted or fired, while other voluntarily sought help to deal with the problem.

Many professional leagues turned to drug testing to determine if players were using illegal drugs. This brought a howl from some civil libertarians and players' unions.

DREW LITTON
Courtesy Rocky Mountain News

BRIAN GABLE
Courtesy Regina Leader–Post (Sask.)

DREW LITTON
Courtesy Rocky Mountain News

BUBBA FLINT
Courtesy Arlington (Tex.) Daily

JEFF KOTERBA
Courtesy Kansas City Star

LARRY WRIGHT
Courtesy Detroit News

JIM BORGMAN
Courtesy Cincinnati Enquirer

"THE KID'S A HOT PROSPECT.... HE'S GOT A GOOD HEAD FOR MERCHANDISING, AN AGENT WHO CAN TAKE YOU DOWNTOWN, AND ONE OF THE BEST URINE SAMPLES I'VE SEEN IN A LONG TIME..."

JOE THIBODEAU
Courtesy Arkansas Democrat

JIM PALMER
Courtesy Montgomery Advertiser

KIRK WALTERS
Courtesy Toledo Blade

DREW LITTON
Courtesy Rocky Mountain News

DAVID WILEY MILLER
Courtesy San Francisco Examiner

BRIAN BASSET
Courtesy Seattle Times

PETER KOHLSAAT
©Modern Times Syndicate

DICK WALLMEYER
Courtesy Independent Press–Telegram
(Calif.)

ADRIAN RAESIDE
Courtesy Times–Colonist (B.C.)

JOE HELLER
Courtesy Green Bay Press-Gazette

SCOTT WILLIS
Courtesy San Jose Mercury-News

JOEL PETT
*Courtesy Lexington
Herald–Leader (Ky.)*

WHILE MS. FRANCKLE CALLS SECURITY, DELLINGSBLAD, ACCOUNTING, THIRD FLOOR, PREPARES TO GIVE HIS FINAL VOLUNTARY URINE SAMPLE

The Big Bertha Of World Menaces

CHARLES WERNER
Courtesy Indianapolis Star

JON KENNEDY
Courtesy Arkansas Democrat

'Can we count on your complete cooperation?'

PHIL BISSELL
Courtesy Lowell (Mass.) Sun

--TASTE OF HIS OWN MEDICINE--

MESSAGE UPDATED!

JOHN MILT MORRIS
© Associated Press

HY ROSEN
Courtesy Albany Times–Union

"C'MON KID, I'LL TAKE YOU IN!"

GEORGE FISHER
Courtesy Arkansas Gazette

JACK HIGGINS
Courtesy Chicago Sun-Times

Kurt Waldheim

For more than 40 years, Kurt Waldheim distinguished himself in the diplomatic service of Austria and even served as secretary-general of the United Nations from 1972 to 1982. For the official record, Waldheim had been careful to portray himself as an Austrian statesman, touching only lightly on his early years. He acknowledged serving in the German army and that while fighting on the Russian front in 1941, he had suffered a leg wound. The injury, he said, excused him from further military service during the war.

In 1986, however, when he campaigned for, and won, the presidency of Austria, a far different picture of his past came to light. Documents uncovered by the World Jewish Congress and other investigators revealed that he was deeply involved with the Nazi movement and with the German death camps. Yugoslavian documents show that he was wanted in connection with "murder, slaughter, shooting of hostages, and ravaging of property by the burning of settlements."

Waldheim vehemently denied all the charges, although he admitted to having given false information in his official biography. He was not brought to trial, although the United Nations War Crimes Commission accused him of similar offenses.

JOSH BEUTEL
Courtesy Saint John
Telegraph–Journal

GARY MARKSTEIN
© Cox Arizona Newspapers

BOB TAYLOR
Courtesy Dallas Times–Herald

YOU KNOW ABOUT ALZHEIMER'S DISEASE. NOW A FRIGHTENING NEW AFFLICTION HAS BEEN DISCOVERED IN AUSTRIA.

WALDHEIMER'S DISEASE

YOU GET OLD AND FORGET YOU WERE A NAZI

UMM... I WAS WITH THE RESISTANCE. THAT'S IT! THE RESISTANCE.

ED STEIN
Courtesy Rocky Mountain News

EXCUSE IT...

AUSTRIA

JEWS

WALDHEIMS NAZI PAST

Unopened foot-locker

JON KENNEDY
Courtesy Arkansas Democrat

BRIAN GABLE
Courtesy Regina Leader–Post (Sask.)

The Kurt Waldheim Story...

"...IT WAS A DARK AND STORMY NIGHT... NO, IT WAS A BRIGHT SUNNY DAY... SORRY, IT WAS CLOUDY WITH INTERMITTENT SHOWERS..."

JIMMY MARGULIES
© *Houston Post*

MARGULIES
©1986 HOUSTON POST
United Feature Syndicate

1944

"SO LONG, WALDHEIM!... AND IF YOU EVER NEED A REFERENCE FOR YOUR RESUMÉ..."

143

STUART CARLSON
Courtesy Milwaukee Sentinel

KURT WALDHEIM—FUHRER ELECT

BILL MITCHELL
Courtesy Potomac News

JERRY ROBINSON
© Cartoonists & Writers Syndicate

. . . and Other Issues

A wide variety of other issues and events claimed the attention of Americans across the nation. William Schroeder, 54, who had become the longest-living recipient of a permanent artificial heart, died on August 6. He had lived 620 days on the plastic-and-metal Jarvic-7 pump. In an effort to upgrade classroom instruction, more and more states were asking teachers to take tests. Teacher associations and unions generally opposed the measures, contending such tests were unnecessary.

The disposal of toxic wastes and the regulation of pesticides were continuing problems. President Reagan signed a bill setting 1993 as the deadline for states to have designated sites for the disposal of low-level radioactive wastes.

The disease AIDS continued as a growing health threat during the year. Surgeon General Everett Koop issued a report urging that all citizens be taught how to protect themselves from AIDS, including school children. The cost of medical care rose 6.7 percent in 1985 while inflation increased only 4.1 percent. When the final figures are in for 1986, it is expected that inflation will be slightly down, but medical costs will still be moving upward.

Noted personalities who died during 1986 included James Cagney, Kate Smith, Roy Cohn, Cary Grant, Benny Goodman, Bill Veeck, Stepin Fechit, and the Duchess of Windsor.

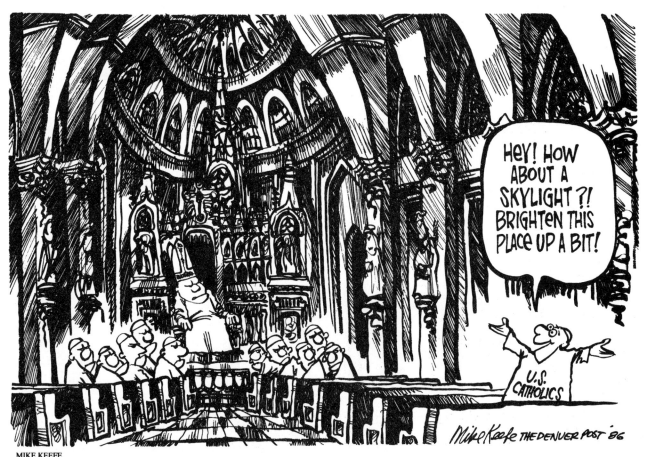

MIKE KEEFE
Courtesy Denver Post

CHARLIE DANIEL
Courtesy Knoxville Journal

DAVID KOLOSTA
Courtesy Houston Post

LINDA BOILEAU
Courtesy Frankfort State Journal

CRAIG MACINTOSH
Courtesy Minneapolis Star–Tribune

JIM DOBBINS
Courtesy Union–Leader

WAYNE STAYSKAL
Courtesy Tampa Tribune

"GUESS THAT EXPLAINS WHY MOST OF MY STUDENTS BEGIN THEIR PAPERS ON EVOLUTION, 'ONCE UPON A TIME...'!"

148

A CONCISE HISTORY OF SEGREGATION

ROBERT DORNFRIED
© Rothco Cartoons

TED TURNER VISITS THE LOUVRE_

CHARLIE DANIEL
Courtesy Knoxville Journal

STEVE LINDSTROM
Courtesy Duluth News–Tribune

GEORGE DANBY
Courtesy Bangor Daily News

150

BERT WHITMAN
Courtesy Phoenix Gazette

JOHN MILT MORRIS
© Associated Press

STEVE ARTLEY
Courtesy Agri News

JOE HELLER
Courtesy Green Bay Press-Gazette

EDDIE GERMANO
Courtesy Brockton Daily Enterprise

JACK JURDEN
*Courtesy Wilmington Evening
Journal–News*

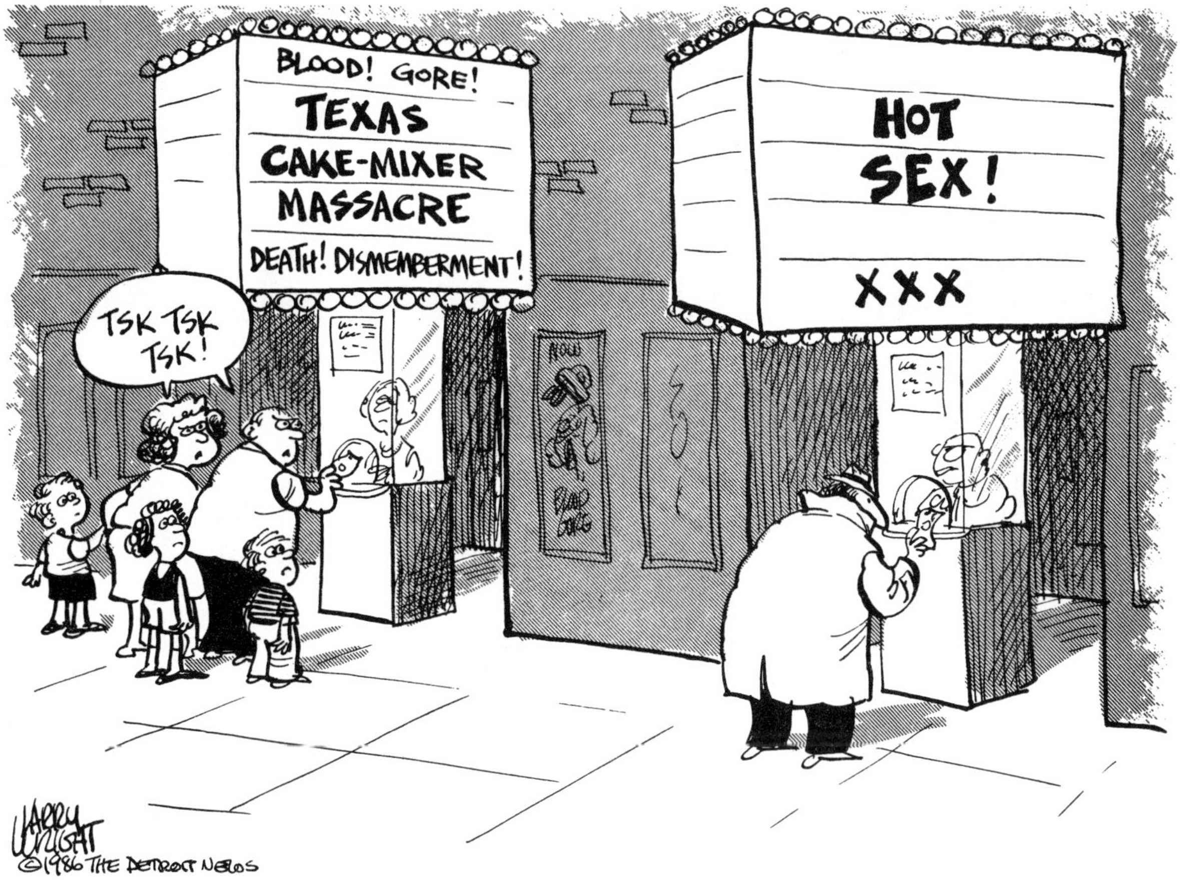
BLOOD! GORE!
TEXAS
CAKE-MIXER
MASSACRE
DEATH! DISMEMBERMENT!
HOT
SEX!
XXX
TSK TSK
TSK!
©1986 THE DETROIT NEWS

LARRY WRIGHT
Courtesy Detroit News

MIKE PETERS
Courtesy Dayton Daily News

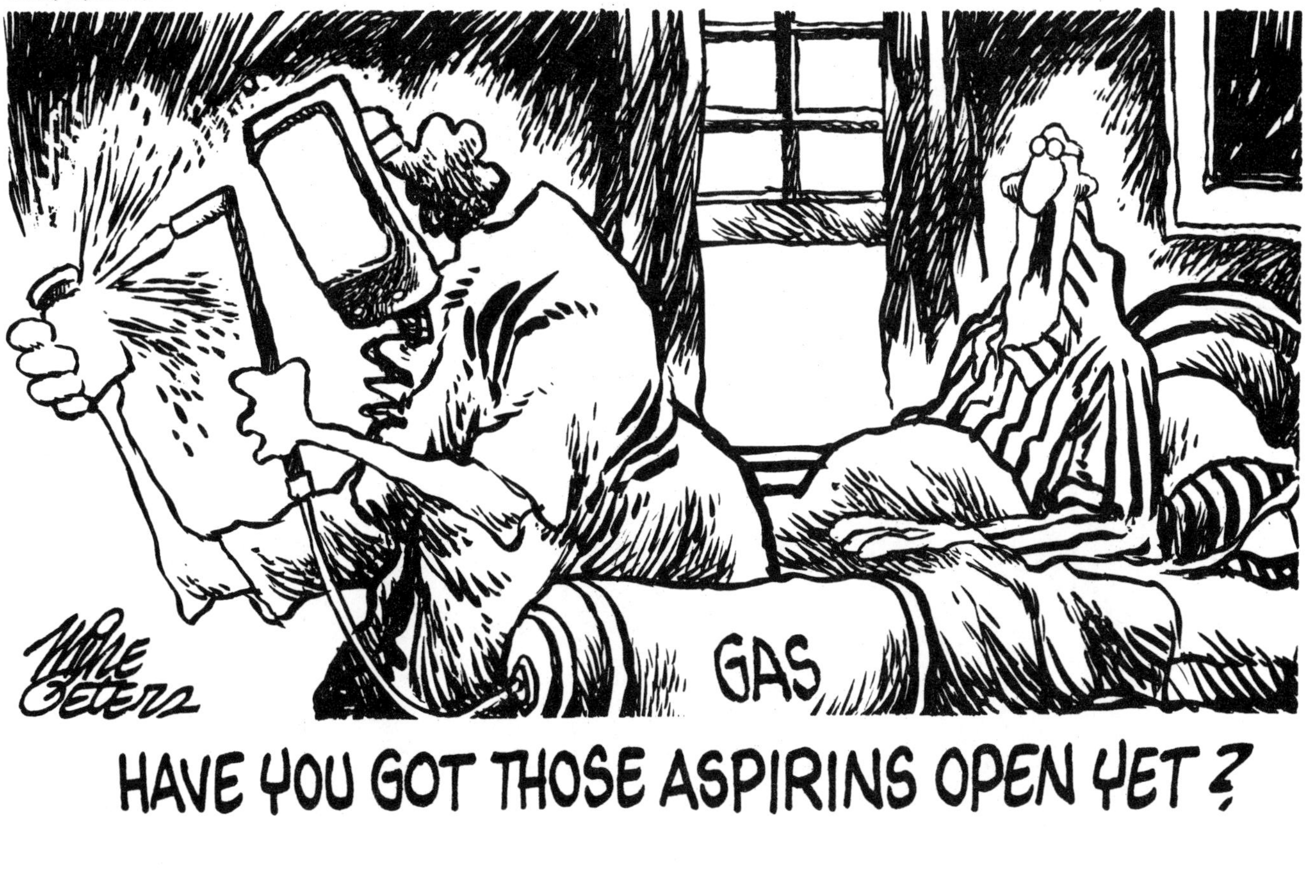
GAS
HAVE YOU GOT THOSE ASPIRINS OPEN YET?

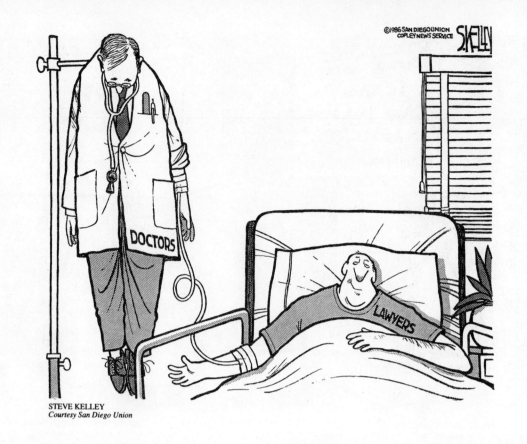

STEVE KELLEY
Courtesy San Diego Union

H. CLAY BENNETT
Courtesy St. Petersburg Times

JEFF STAHLER
Courtesy Cincinnati Post

CRAIG SHELLADY
© Extra Newspaper Features

Sabo
JOURNAL OF
COMMUNICATION
JOSEPH SZABO
© Rothco

FAREWELL JIMMY,
THE YANKEE DOODLE DANDY

MIKE POWELL
Courtesy Paducah Sun

EDDIE GERMANO
Courtesy Brockton Daily Enterprise

Past Award Winners

SIGMA DELTA CHI AWARD EDITORIAL CARTOON

1942—Jacob Burck, Chicago Times
1943—Charles Werner, Chicago Sun
1944—Henry Barrow, Associated Press
1945—Reuben L. Goldberg, New York Sun
1946—Dorman H. Smith, Newspaper Enterprise Association
1947—Bruce Russell, Los Angeles Times
1948—Herbert Block, Washington Post
1949—Herbert Block, Washington Post
1950—Bruce Russell, Los Angeles Times
1951—Herbert Block, Washington Post, and
　　　Bruce Russell, Los Angeles Times
1952—Cecil Jensen, Chicago Daily News
1953—John Fischetti, Newspaper Enterprise Association
1954—Calvin Alley, Memphis Commercial Appeal
1955—John Fischetti, Newspaper Enterprise Association
1956—Herbert Block, Washington Post
1957—Scott Long, Minneapolis Tribune
1958—Clifford H. Baldowski, Atlanta Constitution
1959—Charles G. Brooks, Birmingham News
1960—Dan Dowling, New York Herald-Tribune
1961—Frank Interlandi, Des Moines Register
1962—Paul Conrad, Denver Post
1963—William Mauldin, Chicago Sun-Times
1964—Charles Bissell, Nashville Tennessean
1965—Roy Justus, Minneapolis Star
1966—Patrick Oliphant, Denver Post
1967—Eugene Payne, Charlotte Observer
1968—Paul Conrad, Los Angeles Times
1969—William Mauldin, Chicago Sun-Times
1970—Paul Conrad, Los Angeles Times
1971—Hugh Haynie, Louisville Courier-Journal
1972—William Mauldin, Chicago Sun-Times
1973—Paul Szep, Boston Globe
1974—Mike Peters, Dayton Daily News
1975—Tony Auth, Philadelphia Enquirer
1976—Paul Szep, Boston Globe
1977—Don Wright, Miami News
1978—Jim Borgman, Cincinnati Enquirer
1979—John P. Trever, Albuquerque Journal
1980—Paul Conrad, Los Angeles Times
1981—Paul Conrad, Los Angeles Times
1982—Dick Locher, Chicago Tribune
1983—Rob Lawlor, Philadelphia Daily News
1984—Mike Lane, Baltimore Evening Sun
1985—Doug Marlette, Charlotte Observer

NATIONAL HEADLINERS CLUB AWARD EDITORIAL CARTOON

1938—C.D. Batchelor, New York Daily News
1939—John Knott, Dallas News
1940—Herbert Block, Newspaper Enterprise Association
1941—Charles H. Sykes, Philadelphia Evening Ledger
1942—Jerry Doyle, Philadelphia Record
1943—Vaughn Shoemaker, Chicago Daily News
1944—Roy Justus, Sioux City Journal
1945—F.O. Alexander, Philadelphia Bulletin
1946—Hank Barrow, Associated Press
1947—Cy Hungerford, Pittsburgh Post-Gazette
1948—Tom Little, Nashville Tennessean
1949—Bruce Russell, Los Angeles Times
1950—Dorman Smith, Newspaper Enterprise Association
1951—C.G. Werner, Indianapolis Star
1952—John Fischetti, Newspaper Enterprise Association
1953—James T. Berryman and Gib Crocket, Washington Star
1954—Scott Long, Minneapolis Tribune
1955—Leo Thiele, Los Angeles Mirror-News
1956—John Milt Morris, Associated Press
1957—Frank Miller, Des Moines Register
1958—Burris Jenkins, Jr., New York Journal-American
1959—Karl Hubenthal, Los Angeles Examiner
1960—Don Hesse, St. Louis Globe-Democrat
1961—L.D. Warren, Cincinnati Enquirer
1962—Franklin Morse, Los Angeles Mirror
1963—Charles Bissell, Nashville Tennessean
1964—Lou Grant, Oakland Tribune
1965—Merle R. Tingley, London (Ont.) Free Press
1966—Hugh Haynie, Louisville Courier-Journal
1967—Jim Berry, Newspaper Enterprise Association
1968—Warren King, New York News
1969—Larry Barton, Toledo Blade
1970—Bill Crawford, Newspaper Enterprise Association
1971—Ray Osrin, Cleveland Plain Dealer
1972—Jacob Burck, Chicago Sun-Times
1973—Ranan Lurie, New York Times
1974—Tom Darcy, Newsday
1975—Bill Sanders, Milwaukee Journal
1976—No award given
1977—Paul Szep, Boston Globe
1978—Dwane Powell, Raleigh News and Observer
1979—Pat Oliphant, Washington Star
1980—Don Wright, Miami News
1981—Bill Garner, Memphis Commercial Appeal
1982—Mike Peters, Dayton Daily News
1983—Doug Marlette, Charlotte Observer
1984—Steve Benson, Arizona Republic
1985—Bill Day, Detroit Free Press
1986—Mike Keefe, Denver Post

PULITZER PRIZE
EDITORIAL CARTOON

1922—Rollin Kirby, New York World
1924—J.N. Darling, New York Herald Tribune
1925—Rollin Kirby, New York World
1926—D.R. Fitzpatrick, St. Louis Post-Dispatch
1927—Nelson Harding, Brooklyn Eagle
1928—Nelson Harding, Brooklyn Eagle
1929—Rollin Kirby, New York World
1930—Charles Macauley, Brooklyn Eagle
1931—Edmund Duffy, Baltimore Sun
1932—John T. McCutcheon, Chicago Tribune
1933—H.M. Talburt, Washington Daily News
1934—Edmund Duffy, Baltimore Sun
1935—Ross A. Lewis, Milwaukee Journal
1937—C.D. Batchelor, New York Daily News
1938—Vaughn Shoemaker, Chicago Daily News
1939—Charles G. Werner, Daily Oklahoman
1940—Edmund Duffy, Baltimore Sun
1941—Jacob Burck, Chicago Times
1942—Herbert L. Block, Newspaper Enterprise Association
1943—Jay N. Darling, New York Herald Tribune
1944—Clifford K. Berryman, Washington Star
1945—Bill Mauldin, United Feature Syndicate
1946—Bruce Russell, Los Angeles Times
1947—Vaughn Shoemaker, Chicago Daily News
1948—Reuben L. (Rube) Goldberg, New York Sun
1949—Lute Pease, Newark Evening News
1950—James T. Berryman, Washington Star
1951—Reginald W. Manning, Arizona Republic
1952—Fred L. Packer, New York Mirror
1953—Edward D. Kuekes, Cleveland Plain Dealer
1954—Herbert L. Block, Washington Post
1955—Daniel R. Fitzpatrick, St. Louis Post-Dispatch
1956—Robert York, Louisville Times
1957—Tom Little, Nashville Tennessean
1958—Bruce M. Shanks, Buffalo Evening News
1959—Bill Mauldin, St. Louis Post-Dispatch
1961—Carey Orr, Chicago Tribune
1962—Edmund S. Valtman, Hartford Times
1963—Frank Miller, Des Moines Register
1964—Paul Conrad, Denver Post
1966—Don Wright, Miami News
1967—Patrick B. Oliphant, Denver Post
1968—Eugene Gray Payne, Charlotte Observer
1969—John Fischetti, Chicago Daily News
1970—Thomas F. Darcy, Newsday
1971—Paul Conrad, Los Angeles Times
1972—Jeffrey K. MacNelly, Richmond News Leader
1974—Paul Szep, Boston Globe
1975—Garry Trudeau, Universal Press Syndicate
1976—Tony Auth, Philadelphia Enquirer
1977—Paul Szep, Boston Globe
1978—Jeff MacNelly, Richmond News Leader
1979—Herbert Block, Washington Post

1980—Don Wright, Miami News
1981—Mike Peters, Dayton Daily News
1982—Ben Sargent, Austin American-Statesman
1983—Dick Locher, Chicago Tribune
1984—Paul Conrad, Los Angeles Times
1985—Jeff MacNelly, Chicago Tribune
1986—Jules Feiffer, Universal Press Syndicate

NOTE: Pulitzer was not given 1923, 1936, 1960, 1965, and 1973.

NATIONAL NEWSPAPER
AWARD / CANADA
EDITORIAL CARTOON

1949—Jack Boothe, Toronto Globe and Mail
1950—James G. Reidford, Montreal Star
1951—Len Norris, Vancouver Sun
1952—Robert La Palme, Le Devoir, Montreal
1953—Robert W. Chambers, Halifax Chronicle-Herald
1954—John Collins, Montreal Gazette
1955—Merle R. Tingley, London Free Press
1956—James G. Reidford, Toronto Globe and Mail
1957—James G. Reidford, Toronto Globe and Mail
1958—Raoul Hunter, Le Soleil, Quebec
1959—Duncan Macpherson, Toronto Star
1960—Duncan Macpherson, Toronto Star
1961—Ed McNally, Montreal Star
1962—Duncan Macpherson, Toronto Star
1963—Jan Kamienski, Winnipeg Tribune
1964—Ed McNally, Montreal Star
1965—Duncan Macpherson, Toronto Star
1966—Robert W. Chambers, Halifax Chronicle-Herald
1967—Raoul Hunter, Le Soleil, Quebec
1968—Roy Peterson, Vancouver Sun
1969—Edward Uluschak, Edmonton Journal
1970—Duncan Macpherson, Toronto Daily Star
1971—Yardley Jones, Toronto Star
1972—Duncan Macpherson, Toronto Star
1973—John Collins, Montreal Gazette
1974—Blaine, Hamilton Spectator
1975—Roy Peterson, Vancouver Sun
1976—Andy Donato, Toronto Sun
1977—Terry Mosher, Montreal Gazette
1978—Terry Mosher, Montreal Gazette
1979—Edd Uluschak, Edmonton Journal
1980—Vic Roschkov, Toronto Star
1981—Tom Innes, Calgary Herald
1982—Blaine, Hamilton Spectator
1983—Dale Cummings, Winnipeg Free Press
1984—Roy Peterson, Vancouver Sun
1985—Ed Franklin, Toronto Globe and Mail

Index

INDEX